# The Role of the Church in Aging, Volume III

Programs and Services for Seniors

# The Role of the Church in Aging, Volume III

## Programs and Services for Seniors

Michael C. Hendrickson, MDiv, MTh, PhD
Editor

The Haworth Press
New York • London

*The Role of the Church in Aging, Volume III: Programs and Services for Seniors* has also been published as *Journal of Religion & Aging*, Volume 2, Number 4, Summer 1986.

The Haworth Press, Inc., 12 West 32 Street, New York, NY 10001
EUROSPAN/Haworth, 3 Henrietta Street, London WC2E 8LU England

**Library of Congress Cataloging-in-Publication Data**
(Revised for vol. 3)

The Role of the church in aging.

Vols. 1-2 have also been published as Journal of religion & aging, volume 2, numbers 1/2-3, Fall 1985/Winter 1985-86 and Spring 1986.
Vol. 1 is the proceedings of the National Symposium on the Church and Aging, held in Zion, Ill., Sept. 1984 and sponsored by the Lutheran Council in the USA.
Includes bibliographies and index.
Contents: v. 1. Implications for policy and action—v. 2. Implications for practice and service—v. 3. Programs and services for seniors.
1. Church work with the aged—Congresses. 2. Aged—Congresses. I. Hendrickson, Michael C. II. National Symposium on the Church and Aging (1984 : Zion, Ill.) III. Lutheran Council in the USA.
BV4435.R65       1986         261.8'3426         85-17564
ISBN 0-86656-482-9 (v. 1)
ISBN 0-86656-483-7 (pbk. : v. 1)
ISBN 0-86656-614-7 (v. 2)
ISBN 0-86656-677-5 (v. 3)

# The Role of the Church in Aging

Journal of Religion & Aging
Volume 2, Number 4

## CONTENTS

78245

# The Church as Advocate in Aging

## Betty J. Letzig

**ABSTRACT.** Religious organizations constitute by far the largest single network of voluntary community organizations serving the needs of the elderly in American society. The dramatic increase in the numbers of people 60 years of age and older, which will increase to 500 million by the year 2025, calls for a refocusing of efforts from direct services to a few to advocacy with and in behalf of all older people. The National Interfaith Coalition on Aging has played a major role on the national scene. The World Plan of Action on Aging includes a specific role for non-governmental organizations in the recommendations for implementation on a global scale. The mission of the Church as advocate for the aging has only begun.

Do not cast me off in the time of old age; forsake me not when my strength is spent. For my enemies speak concerning me, those who watch for my life consult together and say, "God has forsaken him; pursue and seize him, for there is none to deliver him." (Psalms 71:9-10)

Truly, I say to you, as you did it to one of the least of these my brethren, you did it to me. (Matthew 25:40)

The mandate is clear—both in the plea from the Psalmist and the words of Christ—the Church has no alternative but to be an "advocate" for the aging.

Religious organizations constitute by far the largest single network of voluntary community organizations serving the needs of the elderly in American society. In the survey of religious affiliations conducted by the Princeton Religion Research Center prior to the 1981 White House Conference on Aging, *only* 3% of persons in the 65-plus age group reported having no religious preference. Given

---

Betty J. Letzig is with the General Board of Global Ministries, National Program Division, The United Methodist Church.

this base, we must acknowledge that with all the churches and synagogues have done, they have failed to live up to either their potential or their responsibilities.

Although religious retirement housing centers constitute the majority of such nonprofit agencies, too much of our attention has been directed to the 5% in institutional settings and too little to the 95% living in the community.

It is just within this past decade that most of the religious bodies have developed policy statements to undergird their ministry to the aging: ministries that include advocacy, direct services, and an educational role with congregations.

One such "Statement on Aging" adopted in 1980 states, in part:

> Older adults in America deserve respect, dignity and equal opportunity. The United Methodist Church is called to be an advocate for the elderly, for their sense of personal identity and dignity, for utilization of experience, wisdom and skills, for health maintenance, adequate income, educational opportunities, and vocational and avocational experiences in cooperation with the public and private sector of society. (Special Task Force of United Methodists, 1980, p. 14)

On an interfaith basis, the National Interfaith Coalition on Aging (NICA), which represents over 30 Protestant, Roman Catholic, Jewish and Orthodox national religious bodies, has as one of its objectives:

> To stimulate cooperative and coordinated action between the nation's religious sector and national secular, private and public organizations and services whose programs and services relate to the welfare and dignity of aging people.

Such statements formed the basis for recommendations from the 1980 NICA-sponsored Mini-Conference on Spiritual and Ethical Value Systems Concerns, including:

> Government guidelines for publicly funded programs must be re-examined to adhere to constitutional provisions. Religious bodies must *not* be discriminated against through an exaggerated concern for or an eccentric definition of separation which excludes any relationships or sense of working together in

common purpose. (National Interfaith Coalition on Aging, 1982, p. 7)

The role of advocates for *all* of society, e.g., the Gray Panther intergenerational concept of linking youth and the aged, finds a natural base within congregations and can be expressed in at least three kinds of roles: (1) the Watchdog Role—being observers in all public arenas to be sure that justice is being done; (2) The Educational Role—teaching so that issues might be faced with full awareness; and (3) The Advocacy-Action Role—working for justice, dignity, and human rights.

Clingan (1975) stated:

> If we enlist the full forces available to us, and this should certainly be the task of men and women of faith, nothing can keep our communities or our nation from achieving its highest dreams for those who so deserve our concern and ministry— THE AGING. (p. 51)

## ADVOCATES IN PUBLIC POLICY

Rabbi Irwin Groner, Chairman of the Synagogue Council of America's Domestic Affairs Committee, in speaking before a committee of the National Conference of Catholic Bishops, said:

> Judaism projects a system of values directing man to serve God by serving his fellowman. The advancement of human welfare is linked with economic security. For this reason religion must address economic institutions, corporate enterprises, and voluntary organizations to help make the economic order meet the basic needs of all our citizens.

The Washington Interreligious Staff Council (WISC), whose members routinely testify before Congressional Committees, regularly addresses the meeting of these basic needs. The Retirement Equity Act, signed by President Reagan in September, 1984, strengthens pension coverage for women. With 71% of older women living in poverty any such breakthrough is a cause for rejoicing—for it did not come easily. One staff member of the United Methodist Women's Division's Washington-based Office of Public

Policy gave virtually full time to that issue for over four years. A continuing issue is that of equal worth/payment.

Other methods of effective legislative advocacy include enabling, through grants, the formation of organizations of older persons who can then speak for themselves. Two of the most effective of these are the Displaced Homemakers Organization and the Older Women's League, both of which were initially funded by church organizations, mostly women's groups.

## ADVOCATES IN SUPPORTIVE SERVICES

### In-Home Services

Churches and synagogues have long been providers of space, both for meetings and "traditional" programs such as senior centers, food and nutrition programs, etc. In more recent years, programs have developed which include "in-home" services. Notable among these are the Shepherd's Center programs, providing comprehensive supportive services; and the newer Interfaith Volunteer Caregivers Program, cosponsored by NICA and the Robert Wood Johnson Foundation which funds it.

In the Interfaith Volunteer Caregivers Program established coalitions, with histories ranging from 18 months to 70 years, are providing leadership in 11 of the projects; with new coalitions having been formed for the remaining 10 projects. Over 600 congregations are involved in the 25 programs, including all of the major Protestant denominations, along with Roman Catholic, Jewish, Eastern Orthodox, Islamic, Buddhist, Bahai and the Nez Pierce Nation's Gathering of the Seven Drums.

First year projections are that more than 9,700 persons will be served by over 6,000 volunteers, who provide not only basic living and personal care services but also special services such as individual needs assessment, service management, caregivers support groups, and hospice.

### Adult Day Care

Increasingly local churches are making available their otherwise under-utilized facilities for adult day care for those with chronic illnesses, which have now become America's major health problem.

These social experiences greatly enhance quality of life beyond what can be provided to a single individual at home, while at the same time providing respite for the caregiver(s). An area of increasing need, and one uniquely the responsibility of the religious bodies, is that of helping caregivers, who frequently suffer from anger and frustration, to find "hope" in their hopeless situations, and to sustain and strengthen them when they tend to draw away from the Church just when they need it most.

## Shelter

Throughout the nation, churches offer floor space to homeless people nightly. But the call to advocacy in their behalf is not just a call to "shelter for the night." The more urgent call is to combat the opposition by businesses and residents who do not want permanent shelters in their neighborhoods. In many areas businesses have closed their restrooms, even to their customers, to prevent the homeless from using them, depriving them of privacy for the most basic of personal needs—elimination.

## Protection

Congressional studies estimate that between 500,000 and one million elders are abused each year. Churches have been quick to assist with the establishment of shelters for battered spouses and children but little has been done to respond to the matter of elder abuse. According to a 1984 study by Christopher Hayes quoted in *Older American Reports* (1984, p. 9): "The typical victim is an ailing woman over 70 who lives alone and depends on relatives to provide care; the typical abusers were adult male children between the ages of 40 and 49." Both fear of retaliation and a natural hesitancy to share their family problems with outsiders prevent abused elders from seeking help.

Since the majority of older persons are related to local congregations, an intentional effort to deal with this issue would render a major service to both the victims and the abusers. Pastors and friendly visitors should be especially alert to indications of abuse whether physical, emotional or financial. Asking questions can help determine need and afford opportunity for referral or the organization of discussion and support groups to help alleviate the causes of abuse. Churches can also help to identify persons who are willing to provide respite care—meeting the needs of both the one providing respite and those in need of such services.

## ADVOCATES IN THE NURTURING
## AND EDUCATIONAL ROLE

The major faiths have long been in the forefront in the provision of social welfare services and agencies/institutions (homes and hospitals) providing care for the aging. National and international organizations have been formed to undergird these programs. But it was 1972 before these bodies came together to deal with the concern for spiritual well-being of the aging—an area of responsibility no other agency has the capability of fulfilling.

### The National Arena

The Administration on Aging urged the religious bodies to respond to the recommendations from the Section on Spiritual Well-Being of the 1971 White House Conference on Aging (WHCOA). The result was the formation in 1972 of the National Interfaith Coalition on Aging (NICA). The four primary objectives of NICA each speak to the unique role of the religious sector. Implementation has included:

1. Development of the definition "spiritual well-being": "Spiritual Well-Being *is* the affirmation of life in a relationship with God, self, community and environment that nurtures and celebrates wholeness."
2. Convening of an Intra Decade Conference on Spiritual Well-Being, and publication of the presentations as a textbook entitled, *Spiritual Well-Being of the Aged.*
3. The two-year Gerontology In Seminary Training (GIST) program which involved more than 100 seminaries in development of course work in the field of gerontology.
4. The 1981 WHCOA Mini-Conference on Spiritual and Ethical Value Systems Concerns.
5. The 1984 Annual Meeting, cosponsored with AARP, on: Concerns About Dying: Ethical and Religious Issues. Topics considered included: Bio-Medical Issues; Theological Values and Ethical Issues; Spiritual Health of the Terminally Ill; Hos-

pice; Public Policy; Alternatives to Long-Term Care; and Church and Family Support Systems.

Decisions about euthanasia are being made every day. NICA is advocating that the churches, not just the courts, have a part in determining public policy on the issue.

NICA continues to press for recognition of the role of spiritual well-being as integral to the provision of public services to the elderly. "A National Interfaith Response to the 1981 White House Conference on Aging" (NICA, 1982) said, in part:

> The national policy articulated in the report appears to be directed almost solely to the current economic and political climate. It is not a long-range policy statement. Furthermore, it stresses physical requirements of the elderly at the expense of emotional needs, ignoring the proven relationship between physical and emotional health, which ultimately has significant social and economic consequences. Concern for the whole person is both cost-effective and morally correct. We strongly affirm the constitutional formula for the relationship of church and state: the official functions of the state must not be interlocked with the official or institutional functions of any church or synagogue. These two entities must be kept institutionally separate. The constitution, however, leaves room for moral, spiritual, political, and administrative interaction and for responsive teamwork. WHCOA delegate recommendations and other official conference documents provide a number of examples in which such team work may be highly effective without violating the separation principle.

Among the 668 recommendations adopted by the WHCOA more than 50 are relevant to the religious sector role. These include:

> #219. Be it further resolved that a blue-ribbon panel . . . be appointed by the Secretary of HHS to originate and disseminate, consistent with the First Amendment provision of the Constitution, both the concept of spiritual well-being, as a valid part of human wholeness, and strategies for more effective integration of the religious sector into the total continuum of aging programs and support services. (p. 123)

#374. Just like other professional groups, the expertise and input of the clergy should be utilized by both government and the private sector in a comprehensive approach to the training of professionals and non-professionals in the planning, implementing and evaluation of programs and in facilities and resources for older Americans. (p. 147)

#478. The aging network at all levels should include religious organizations and congregations as partners in their planning and delivery of services, encouraging these bodies to survey the elderly and project programs for meeting their needs. (p. 173)

Recommendations from the WHCOA Mini-Conference on Spiritual and Ethical Value Systems Concerns likewise reinforce the collaborative roles of the religious bodies and government:

1. Model or pilot programs should be designed to implement wholistic well-being approaches. (p. 4)
2. Churches and synagogues should be among the agencies allowed to administer tax-funded projects for the elderly. Religious groups will thus become more productive in their natural roles as care providers. (p. 4)
3. Tax funds should be provided for the education of professionals, including religious professionals, in the fields of gerontology and geriatrics. (p. 8)
4. Public and private sector should collaborate on a massive educational effort aimed at the eradication of ageism and the fear of aging in American society. They should lift-up accurate and positive images of aging, ultimately making possible a realistic consideration of need-entitlement, as opposed to age-entitlement, as a basis for policy. (p. 11)

NICA has taken seriously the statement of the noted gerontologist, Dr. David Moberg, that most textbooks, monographs, professional articles, and other resources used by gerontologists ignore or greatly downplay the role of religion. Board members active in the Western Gerontological Society have worked to have the role of religion recognized. This has resulted in: (1) A special track on Religion and Aging in the annual meetings; (2) The creation of a Standing Committee on Religion and Aging; (3) The 1983 special issue of *Generations*, on "Religion and Aging"; and (4) Plans for a 1986 two-day post-conference institute on "Dimensions of Spiritual Well-Being" to be cosponsored by WGS and NICA.

NICA also cosponsored with the Third Age Center of Fordham University and Opera Pia International a one-day pre-conference session on "Religion and the Images of Aging" for the International Gerontological Society in New York City in July, 1985.

## The Global Arena

U.N. demographic projections show the worldwide 60 and older population increasing 224% between 1975 and 2025, while an increase of only 102% is predicted for the total worldwide population during that same period. By that same year, approximately 72% of the elderly (the majority of whom will be women) will reside in developing nations, compared to roughly 52% at the present. An additional major shift is that the majority of those will be in urban rather than rural areas, with the result that the families as traditional caregivers will, with that urbanization, no longer be available.

Religious bodies have a major role in this global arena. At the U.N. World Assembly on Aging in 1982, as Non-Governmental Organization (NGO) representatives, they were able to negotiate with delegates to obtain significant amendments to the Draft of the World Plan of Action on Aging at three specific points:

> Par. 25(c)—The phrase "discrimination based on race, sex or religion" was substituted for a reference to "racial discrimination." (p. 53)

> Par. 25(i)—Added terms "religious" and "spiritual" to the principle: "Preparation of the entire population for the later stages of life should be an integral part of social policies and encompass physical, psychological, cultural, *religious, spiritual*, economic, health and other factors"; (p. 54)

> Par. 32—The statement, "Since spiritual well-being is as important as material well-being, all policies, programs and activities should be developed to support and strengthen spiritual well-being of the aging. Governments should guarantee the freedom of religious practices and expressions," (p. 57) was included in the goals and policy recommendations for action.

*Implementation*

For the first time, a U.N. document includes a specific role for NGO's:

> Par. 99—Governments, national and local non-governmental voluntary organizations are urged to join in the cooperative effort to accomplish the objectives of the Plan. . . . Governments are also urged to encourage and, where possible, support national and private organizations dealing with matters concerning the elderly and the aging of the population. (p. 80)

One immediate response was the publication by the Office of Family Education of the World Council of Churches of *The Church and The Aging in a Changing World* (Boggs, 1982), which highlights from the reports submitted to the World Assembly on Aging the roles of churches in various countries. Opera Pia International is continuing its world-wide efforts in behalf of the aging and the Baptist World Alliance has placed special emphasis on the plight of older persons in their program of disaster relief and refugee work.

Churches, because of their role in worldwide health care through their mission programs, have a key role to play in the achievement of the World Health Organization goal of "Health For All by the Year 2000." Dr. Sylvia Talbot, member of the WCC Christian Medical Commission, speaking at a United Methodist sponsored symposium on "A Woman's Health is More Than A Medical Issue" in New York City, in 1983, called health a value and vision for the world; adding that health is the means by which we pursue things of value. One direct result of that symposium was that the issue of older women's health was on the agenda for the 1985 U.N. End of Decade World Conference for Women—a major achievement since the concerns of older women were virtually ignored in the two preceding conferences.

Such emphasis on the particular needs of the aging in the area of health care is critical in light of the 1982 responses by developing countries to the U.N.'s "Fifth Population Inquiry Among Governments" which show no evidence of any effort to integrate the older population into basic health services or into preventive health plans.

Dr. Arthur S. Flemming, formerly Commissioner on Aging, continually challenges the Churches to make certain that church members never rest on their laurels but continue throughout their lives to serve their God through continued advocacy for all of society. As "advocate in aging" the task of the Churches has only begun.

## REFERENCES

Clingan, Donald F. *Aging persons in the community of faith.* Indianapolis: Indiana Commission on the Aging and the Aged, 1975.

*Final report the 1981 White House Conference on Aging.* Vol. 3: Recommendations, Post-Conference Survey of Delegates.

*National Interfaith Coalition on Aging: 1972 Articles of Incorporation.* Athens, Ga.: National Interfaith Coalition on Aging, 1982.

*National Symposium: Spiritual and ethical value system concerns.* Athens, Ga.: National Interfaith Coalition on Aging, 1980.

*Older American Reports.* Vol. 8, No. 23. Arlington, Va.: Capitol Publications, Inc. June 8, 1984.

*Report of the World Assembly on Aging.* New York: United Nations, 1982. A/Conf. 113/31.

*Study/Action statement on aging for use by the United Methodist Church at all levels.* Prepared by a Special Task Force of United Methodists. Cincinnati, Oh.: General Board of Global Ministries, 1980.

# Churches as Geriatric Health Clinics for Community Based Elderly

## Sandra L. Hendrickson

**ABSTRACT.** In most communities there are significant numbers of elderly, especially females who are frail, widowed and live alone. They generally make insufficient use of traditional health care services oftentimes because of location outside of immediate neighborhoods, high costs and perceived disinterest of many providers to their unique needs. Many current models for delivering health care do not consider the multi-functional needs of this population. A model is presented in which several geriatric health clinics are housed in neighborhood churches and use Geriatric Nurse Practitioners as the primary care providers. Care is directed toward management of chronic illness and maximizing the capacity of the elderly to function independently in the community. Volunteers from the parishes and community are trained to provide staff support for the clinic operations and to perform the follow-up activities on personal care aspects of the frail and vulnerable elderly. Local parishes serve as satellites and are linked to a long term care facility which provides administrative and clinical support as well as an integrated care system.

There is mounting concern by policymakers and clinicians regarding the increasing numbers of frail and disabled elderly who are living in urban communities. Many are living on the verge of imminent institutionalization because of physical, psychological and social dysfunction. The numbers of frail and disabled elderly, those persons over 75 years of age with chronic diseases and functional disabilities are growing more rapidly than any other age group. Of the 25 million persons over 65 years of age, approximately 9 million are over 75 years of age. Projections are that by 2010, there will be 15 million frail elderly; 10 million of those will be females (Federal Council on Aging, 1978).

After 75 years of age, over 50% of all the elderly have one or

---

Sandra L. Hendrickson is with Mount St. Mary's College, Department of Nursing.

*13*

more chronic diseases or functional disabilities which threaten to limit independent living. The reality is that, now, or in the near future, these elderly will require increased monitoring of their chronic diseases and assistance with daily living in order to remain in their homes. Remaining at home has been shown to be more satisfying, less costly and more appropriate than institutionalized care.

The elderly comprise 11% of the population but use over 29% of the health care dollar (Federal Council on Aging, 1978). Obviously, future projections are for health care costs to increase. If the same health care delivery systems pervade in the future, by 1990 expenditures for all traditional health care services will increase four times over (Federal Council on Aging, 1978).

Future projections suggest a preponderance of female frail elderly. According to Dr. Robert Butler, "The problems of aging are so much the problems of women." He has called this the century of older women (Keys, 1980, p. 9). Of the women who are 75 years and older, approximately 41% are living alone and widowed (Federal Council on Aging, 1978). Increased mobility, decreased family size and increased longevity have been factors related to the large numbers of females who are living alone with limited financial, social and personal resources. Clearly, most women can expect, at some time in their lives, to be widowed and alone, a life-style for which many older women are unprepared.

Recognizing the imperative to create solutions to handle an increasing number of frail elderly, the escalating costs for institutionalization and the demand by the elderly for solutions to increase quality of life, policymakers and public agencies at all levels have begun to support, conceptually and financially, innovative models for community-based long-term care. This paper describes a model for providing health care to the frail and disabled elderly, particularly women, in which churches and a long-term care institution are used as places for delivery of health services. The model uses the Geriatric Nurse Practitioner as the primary service provider with support of volunteers from parishes, a long-term care institution and existing service agencies in the target area.

## BACKGROUND

Information is presented on the use of community based health and social services by the elderly, particularly women; the Geriatric

Nurse Practitioner as an appropriate provider of primary care to the elderly; and previous projects which have been successful in providing services to the elderly so they can live independently in their neighborhoods.

## Use of Services

There is increasing recognition that making services available for the elderly does not mean that they will use them. Recent research by Krout (1984) indicates there is lack of participation by frail elderly in many programs designed to serve them. The elderly are more likely to use health services than programs which are primarily social, psychological or financial in nature. Health services are typically used when elderly persons have symptoms or diminished physical functioning (Wan & Odell, 1981; Evashwick, Rowe, Diehr & Branch, 1984). Further, if the elderly client has a regular source of health care there is increased likelihood that other health and social services will also be used.

Lack of knowledge about the existence and availability of programs is another factor effecting the low use of services for the elderly. This has been particularly true of community-based services. Krout (1984) reported that while elderly knew of medical and hospital services in their neighborhoods, there was virtually no knowledge about home health, homemaker and information/referral services. These services are more likely to facilitate the elderly to remain in their homes rather than be institutionalized. Because of lack of knowledge and use of community-based services, many elderly seek assistance from known traditional providers. Physicians, emergency rooms, hospitals and nursing homes are often used for treatment of stable chronic disease and social/psychological problems even when more appropriate, less costly, and more accessible community-based services are available (Wan, Odell & Lewis, 1982). Wan and Odell (1981) found that frail elderly with higher levels of psychological dysfunctioning, difficulty in performing activities of daily living and high users of social services tended to have larger numbers of physician visits as well. These studies suggest the elderly need assistance both in assessing their service needs and in selecting the most accessible, low cost and appropriate care.

Gender is a factor related to the use of service programs by the frail elderly. Generally women tend to use more health and social services than men (Verbrugge, 1981; Wan & Odell, 1981; Krout,

1983). Verbrugge (1981) suggests that women use more services because they have increased acute illnesses and are more aware of their physiological changes as well as more experienced in attending to health care needs having done so for members of their families. Despite these findings, others indicate that elderly women are oftentimes thwarted in their attempts to use the current health care systems. Many physician providers lack understanding of the multiple body changes that occur with aging, particularly related to women's health. They also display poor attitudes about aging by dismissing symptoms or by treating chronic and social/psychological problems as though they were acute illnesses (Pedrin, 1980).

Type, nature and location of services have been other factors related to use of health services by the elderly. Wan, Odell & Lewis (1982) studied 2,000 noninstitutionalized older persons living in low-income urban areas near five different neighborhood health centers. Elderly in the neighborhood increased their use of services by a factor of three in comparison to a similar group of elderly outside of the neighborhood. Ingman and Lawson (1982) assert that the elderly need not only more services, but that they need specialized health services focused to their needs. Many elderly indicate that the current service delivery models present obstacles to meeting their multi-dimensional needs. The specialist-oriented, acute care, hospital-based system oftentimes produces iatrogenic effects for elderly persons seeking care for chronic conditions and social/psychological or environmental problems.

## Geriatric Nurse Practitioner as Primary Care Provider for the Elderly

The use of nurse practitioners as providers of primary care services is based on their potential to improve access and to lower costs without compromising quality. Nurse practitioners have both a substitutive and complementary relationship to other providers of health care. Studies identifying services provided by nurse practitioners have shown that they can provide up to 80% of the primary medical services normally provided by a physician. Coulehan and Sheehy (1978) found that nurse practitioners were trained in diagnosis and treatment of chronic diseases such as heart disease and arthritis, psychophysiologic reactions and acute self-limiting conditions. In addition, nurse practitioners emphasized prevention, maintenance counseling, health promotion and related activities more often than physicians.

Nurse practitioners initially were created to improve access to primary care for underserved populations in rural and inner city areas. Their impact can be evaluated on the degree to which their presence increases use of services and the extent of consumer acceptance. Chambers (1977) studied the impact of nurse practitioners on patterns of care in rural Newfoundland. After a year, there was a significant shift toward community-based care rather than hospital or outpatient clinic services. Also, there was a 5% decrease in hospitalization for nurse practitioner patients compared to a 39% increase in hospitalization for physician patients. Consumers have generally felt positive about the services of the nurse practitioner. Support for and satisfaction levels have increased in each instance where nurse practitioners have been employed.

If nurse practitioners are to provide a real substitution for physician providers, then the impact of care as measured by patient outcomes must also be evaluated. Bessman (1974) reported on patient outcomes after two years in a nurse practitioner run diabetic ambulatory clinic. This study compared the impact of care between nurse practitioners and senior house physicians for 500 diabetic patients of all ages. No statistical difference in patient outcomes such as blood sugar and blood urea nitrogen levels, deaths and hospitalization rates were reported between nurse practitioners and physicians. In addition, the study noted that nurse practitioners had better continuity of care, more emphasis on education and a decrease in broken appointment rates. Some nine years later, nurse practitioners continued to function effectively in this clinic. Runyan (1977) found similar results for patients in a Tennessee ambulatory care clinic which specialized in cardiac and hypertensive conditions. Other studies report similar results in patient outcomes when nurse practitioners are used as primary providers of care (Kane et al., 1975; Gordon & Issacs, 1977; Sackett et al., 1974).

A further impetus for promoting nurse practitioners as primary care providers is the opportunity to lower costs of health care (Neumann, 1983). Either costs to consumers are actually reduced or, as in most cases, benefits accrue to institutional providers or to physicians (Prescott & Driscoll, 1980; Edmunds, 1980; Freund and Overstreet, 1981). Burnip et al. (1976) studied the impact of six nurse practitioners by comparing their cost per visit with those of physicians and reported a 36% reduction in costs. Most studies of nurse practitioners which have included a cost comparison analysis have been on practices where the nurse practitioner functioned as an extension rather than a substitute for physician services. Thus, real reductions in cost of unit per service are likely artificially suppressed. Still, Merenstein, Wolfe, and Barker (1974) reported a 3.3% increase for patient costs as compared to 25.4% for patients receiving care from a physician.

Geriatric Nurse Practitioners (GNP) grew out of concerns for more fully responding to the multiplicity of needs which the elderly present. Morgan (1977), in commenting on the role of the Geriatric Nurse Practitioner, stated that in long-term care settings,

> They (GNP's) are uniquely trained and skilled to do what very few physicians will ever be able to do and they should be looked upon not only as a substitute for a physician, but the ideal person responsible for health care.

According to Ebersole (1983), GNP's are the most important health professionals to coordinate the health care of the elderly. Their holistic approach to health care, a background in nursing, an orientation towards addressing the social psychological needs of the elderly as well makes them a vital alternative to serving as the primary care provider for the elderly.

The Mountain States Health Corporation, under a Kellogg Foundation three year grant, prepared GNP's to function as primary care providers in long-term care settings. Preliminary reports have cited the following benefits of having a GNP as primary care provider in long-term care settings: (1) reduction in transfer to acute care facilities; (2) less reliance on medications, restraints and continence devices; (3) decreased mortality; (4) more returns to community living; and (5) increased patient and family satisfaction. Expansion of this concept to day care, home care, and ambulatory clinics is expected in the future.

### Models for Ambulatory Care for the Elderly

In recent years several model projects in delivering ambulatory care to the elderly have demonstrated positive impact for lowering the cost of care while improving the appropriateness of services. TRIAGE, a model project in Connecticut, was designed to provide a single entry assessment mechanism and coordination for delivering institutional, ambulatory and in-home services to the elderly. The features of the model which have accounted for its effectiveness include: (1) Providing whatever service was deemed necessary for the elderly person rather than fitting the needs of the elderly client into a defined list of available services; (2) Using an integrated service delivery system which functions at the local level and thereby optimizes the available resources; and (3) Increasing the accuracy of assessment and problem identification because of using the broker case management model. Preliminary results indicate that the elderly of TRIAGE increased their use of health and social services and independent living. However, costs for care increased but were proportionately less when the increased service use was accounted for (Hicks, Raisz, Segal & Doherty, 1981).

ACCESS, The Assessment for Community Care Services program of Monroe County Long Term Care Program in upstate New York, has been addressing the problem of inappropriate utilization of health care institutions. The project provides assessment, case management, and ongoing monitoring. ACCESS's referral system has successfully placed elderly in appropriate levels of care. At the same time, ACCESS has demonstrated a decrease in cost where five days of nursing home care is equivalent to ten days of home care. Gaining a data base for identifying problems related to long-term care is another outcome of ACCESS (Eggert, 1982).

Another ACCESS project is a Robert Wood Johnson demonstration directed towards understanding the relative attributes of the direct assessment versus brokerage model of case management. The experimental model for this project incorporates a direct assessment function with case management as well as providing some services directly. The multidisciplinary case management team consists of community health nurses, social workers and case aides. The team operates within a specifically defined catchment area and must work within a prescribed budget. One of the study hypotheses is that a change in authorization for services and incentives for case managers would result in cost reductions and in greater use of informal supports. Findings for the first eight months suggest that cost for services was reduced by 12%. There was also a decrease in use of hospital days, transportation, registered nurse and licensed vocational nurse visits, home health aides and homemaker services. However, nursing home days, physician visits and community health nurse/social worker/case manager visits increased. The patterns that emerged were consistent with the project goals. More informal support was used and therefore less trained in-home assistance. Decreased hospitalization was related to patients leaving the hospital sooner and needing more physician or nursing home care immediately after discharge (Eggert, 1984).

In summary, the literature clearly reveals that current approaches to health care for the elderly are highly suspect as being both inadequate and in many cases, inappropriate. The highly specialized, technology dominated and acute oriented health system is not only costly but, some have suggested, a dangerous system to the elderly who depend upon it for assistance. The primary environments of hospitals, medical clinics and outpatient clinics are not conducive for improving access for many frail community-based elderly. Physicians are the primary decision makers for patient care within these more acute care oriented environments. All of these factors serve to drive up costs, create unnecessary dependence on formal care-givers, emphasize the wrong type of services for the elderly, restrict access, and in some cases, create iatrogenic effects. The fact that these issues have begun to be realized by a growing number of policymakers, long-term care administrators and gerontologists, is evidenced by attempts to provide geriatric health and social services within neighborhood settings which make use of providers of care who are specially trained to meet the multidimensional needs of the frail elderly.

While not conclusive, the TRIAGE and ACCESS demonstrations suggest that community-based programs which include assessment, health and social care monitoring, supportive care by both informal and formal care-givers can provide appropriate services, control costs, improve access without any significant reduction in the quality of care given to the elderly. All of the models tested so far have employed a multidisciplinary team approach which incorporated the services of a social worker, nurse, physician and others as members of the primary assessment team. While this approach serves to increase the level to which services required are both identified and delivered in a more coherent less fragmented fashion resulting in more appropriate care for the elderly, it has not demonstrated significant reductions in overall costs. And where costs may have genuinely been reduced, the fact that these savings accrued as a benefit to the sponsoring institutions and/or physicians involved would suggest that these savings would not be fully recognized under present study conditions.

## DESCRIPTION OF THE GERIATRIC HEALTH CLINICS

This model, one that has not been sufficiently tested, is one that utilizes geriatric nurse practitioners skilled at conducting interdisciplinary health and psychosocial assessments within community-based settings and which is staffed by volunteers who also provide follow-up and ongoing supportive activities. This model would reduce the numbers of providers needed especially in primary assessment activities. Further, given the resources of volunteers to serve as support staff for the geriatric health clinics as well as trained to provide informal care, follow-up and support activities for disabled elderly, these services can most likely be handled in a more cost efficient way. Finally, by utilizing familiar neighborhood settings such as churches and synagogues, this approach will serve to enhance a more appropriate inclusion of informal caregivers in the follow-up and supportive activities for the vulnerable elderly and increase access for those elderly who currently represent an underserved population.

### Organizational Components

The primary organizational components are the following: (1) Churches which are (a) located in a population targeted with a density of frail elderly (especially women); (b) house health clinics; and (c) provide operational, supportive, and follow-up activities through parish and community volunteers; (2) The Geriatric Nurse Practitioner Corporation which has contractual relationships with the long-term care institution to manage and service the health clinics located in both the parishes and the long-term care facility; and (3) The multi-level long-term care corporation which houses one of five geriatric clinics and also provides administrative and medical support for the overall operations.

Why use churches for geriatric health clinics? Churches are institutions which current elderly have been socialized to as a setting that is a supportive and familiar one in which they have experienced both love and concern from others. The churches' orientation to the wholeness of persons complements the multi-dimensional needs of the elderly. Further, most churches are located within neighborhoods where the frail elderly live. Finally, churches have people and resources which are often underutilized. The ease of access combined with the supportive atmosphere makes churches and syna-gogues natural and refreshing entry points for geriatric health care. Volunteers of all ages from the parishes and community are used to assist in the operations of the clinic and with supportive and follow-up services within the homes of the elderly. In the clinic, volunteers set up the equipment, complete intake information, assist with assessments and serve as friends to the patients. Supportive services which the elderly need are designed around home manage-ment, personal care and social support services (Scharer, 1984). Services are created to meet the unique needs of each elderly per-son. Using volunteers allows for flexibility in both the kinds of ser-vices as well as the times for providing them. Within each parish, a volunteer leader serves to coordinate the services.

Another major component of this model is the Geriatric Nurse Practitioner Corporation which manages the overall operations and staff for the clinics. Key management functions include: (1) negotia-tions with parish leaders for space, equipment, volunteer recruit-ment and training, and insurance and liability clearances; (2) promoting the clinic to the parish to secure volunteers and a network of known frail and disabled elderly with no regular health care pro-vider; (3) securing Geriatric Nurse Practitioners to provide assess-ments and follow-up care and a full-time coordinator of volunteer services; and (4) securing start up funding and mechanisms to assure the financial health and continuation of the clinics.

The Geriatric Nurse Practitioners who are providing primary care to the elderly will perform complete assessments that gather in-formation about the history and current status of physical, psycho-logical, social and environmental problems. The GNP designs a plan of care which uses the person's optimal capacity and existing informal caregivers as much as possible. This care plan is imple-mented under the direction of the GNP and in conjunction with selected volunteers. Follow-up health care is provided to the elderly for conditions which are primarily stable chronic diseases. The GNP consults with the medical director in the long-term care insti-tution for situations which are more acute and complex. A referral network of physicians and social agencies in the target area is avail-able when needed.

The third major organizational component in the model is the multi-level long-term care corporation which serves as the sponsor-ing organization for the GNP corporation. In exchange for sponsor-ship conditions, the long-term care corporation acquires: (1) the services of the GNP corporation to provide health services on site for residents as well as creating referral linkages to the community through the church-based clinics; (2) increased visibility in the community, a source for future residents; (3) increased growth potential in the new link of the long-term care continuum; and (4) increased financial base because of increased third-party reimbursements.

Through the long-term care corporation, the GNP clinic group have an administrative structure for billing for third-party reimbursement and contracting for services of the medical director. Currently, in many states, GNP's can provide medical care through protocols. Protocols are legitimized when they are created by an interdisciplinary team of nurse practitioners, physicians and others. Further, the medical director of the long term care corporation serves as a consultant for patient management problems and a referral for unstable and acute problems. In addition, the long-term care corporation provides office space for centralized communication, scheduling of patients for the clinics and coordinating volunteer services.

## REFERENCES

Bessman, A. (1974). Comparison of medical care in nurse clinician and physician clinics in medical school affiliated hospitals. *Journal of Chronic Disease, 27,* 115-125.

Burnip, R. (1976). Well-child care by pediatric nurse practitioners in a large group practice. *American Journal of Disabled Child, 130,* 51-56.

Chambers, L., Bruce-Lockart, P., Black, D., Sampson, E. & Burke, M. (1977). A controlled trial of the impact of the family practice nurse on volume, quality and cost of rural health services. *Medical Care, 15,* 971-981.

Coulehan, J. C. & Sheedy, S. (1978). The role, training, and one year's experience of a medical nurse practitioner. *Health Service, 88*(8), 27-29.

Ebersole, P. (1982). Roles and functions of GNP's in Long Term Care as viewed by physician, nurse practitioner and administrator. *American Health Care Association Journal, 8*(2), 2-7.

Edmunds, M. (1980). Financial concerns of nurse practitioners. *Nurse Practitioner, 33,* 50-51.

Eggert, G. M. & Brodows, B. S. (1982). The ACCESS process: Assuring quality in long term care. In R. E. Bennett, S. A. Frisch, B. J. Gurland & D. Wilder, (Eds.) *Coordinated service delivery systems for the elderly—new approaches for care and referral in New York State.* (pp. 35- 46). New York: Hawthorne Press.

Eggert, G. M. & Brodows, B. S. (1984). Direct assessment vs. brokerage: A comparison of care management models. Unpublished manuscript. Monroe County Long Term Care Program.

Evashwick, C., Rowe, G., Diehr, P. & Branch, L. (1984). Factors explaining the use of health care services by the elderly. *Health Services Research, 19*(3), 357-382.

Federal Council on Aging Chartbook (1978). U.S. Department of Health and Social Services of the Council on Aging, Washington, D.C.

Freund, C. M. & Overstat, G. N. The economic potential of nurse practitioners. *Nurse Practitioner, 28*,32,36,55.

Gordon, K. & Isaacs, G. (1977). Nurses staffed decentralized care of diabetes at Frontier Nursing Service: Clinical unknowns. In A. Bliss & E. Cohen (Eds), *The New Health Professionals.* Germantown, Md: Aspen Systems Corp.

Hicks, B., Raisz, H., Segal, J. & Doherty, N. (1981). The TRIAGE experiment in coordinated care for the elderly. *American Journal of Public Health, 71,* (9), 991-1001.

Ingman, S. R. & Lawson, I. R. (1982). Utilization of specialized ambulatory care by the elderly. *Medical Care, 20*(3), 331-338.

Kane, R. L., Jorgenson, L. A., Teteberg, B., Kuwahara, J. (1975). Is good nursing home care feasible? *Journal of the American Medical Association, 235,* (5), 516-519.

Keys, N. (1980). The elderly majority; unique resources and unique needs. *Generations, 4*(6), 9,35.

Krout, J. A. (1983). Knowledge and use of services by the elderly: A critical review of the literature. *International Journal of Aging and Human Development, 17*(2), 153-167.

Krout, J. A. (1984). Use of services by the elderly. *Social Service Review, 3*(2), 281-290.

Morgan, W. A. (1977). *Proceedings of the 3rd North American symposium on long term care administration.* Washington, D.C.: American College of Nursing Home Administrators.

Neumann, B. R. (1983). Cost-effectiveness issues and research studies. *Journal Of Long Term Care Administration, 2*(3), 48-53.

Pedrin, V. & Brown, S. (1980). Sexism and ageism: Obstacles to health care for women. *Generations, 4*(4), 20-21.

Prescott, P. A. & Driscoll, L. (1980). Evaluating nurse practitioner performance. *Nurse Practitioner, 33,* 52-54.

Scharer, L. K. (1984). Volunteers in long-term care: an overview. In P. A. Feinstein, M. Gornick & J. Greenberg (Eds.). *Long-term care financing and delivery systems: Exploring some alternatives.,* pp. 117-123. Conference proceedings. Health Care Financing Administration, Washington, D.C.: U.S. Department of Health and Social Services.

Verbrugge, L. M. (1981). Women and men: Mortality and health of older people. In B. B. Hess & K. Bond, (Eds.), *Leading Edges: recent research on older people and psychosocial aging.* Washington, D.C.: National Institute on Aging, U.S. Department of Health and Human Services.

Wan, T. H. & Odell, B. G. & Lewis, D. T. (1982). *Promoting the well-being of the elderly: A community diagnosis.* New York: Hawthorne Press.

Wan, T. H. & Odell, R. G. (1981). Factors affecting the use of social and health services among the elderly. *Aging and Society, 1*(1), 95-114.

# Day Centers for Older Adults: Parish and Agency Partnership

Joanne Negstad
Roger Arnholt

**ABSTRACT.** As a relatively new service concept which addresses the care of the frail older adult, Day Centers offer a rare opportunity for the partnership of local parishes and service agencies. In typical local parishes, there is a vast increase in the number of frail older adults as well as the number of their care-giving families. Day Centers offer an opportunity for wholistic care for the older adults. By careful programing the needs of the whole person are addressed: social, physical, emotional, and spiritual. Care-giving families appreciate sharing their responsibility. Parishes have vast resources to offer Day Centers. Agencies have the expertise for program development and operations. With the partnership of parish and agency, resources are enhanced. Benefited are the older adults served, the parish, the agency and the community.

## DAY CENTERS FOR OLDER ADULTS: A CONCEPTUAL FRAMEWORK

Recent population statistics tell us that in the next 40 years we will see the population over 60 years of age double. In the very old population (over 85) we will see 3 times as many people in the next 40 years.

Reflect for a moment on your own experience in your family and relationships. Remember your knowledge of a frail older person whose increased dependency on the family for care affects the total family system. Remember the agony of facing the decision of institutionalization of that dear older person. Think of the mixture of

Joanne Negstad and Roger Arnholt are with Lutheran Social Services of Illinois.

This paper presented at the National Symposium on The Church and Aging, Zion, Illinois, September, 1984.

25

78245

patience/impatience, love/anger, willingness to serve/physical fatigue.

Visualize the parish to which you currently belong. Note the names in the church bulletins of those members who are being cared for in institutions. Think of the conversations among other parish members about the needs of frail older family members. As you walk in the rooms of your church building, picture an area usable for caring for those older friends who may be struggling with the effects of diminishing sight or hearing, stroke, diabetes, memory loss, or social isolation.

Day Centers for older adults is a relatively new service concept. Often it is called "Day Care." We are cautious about using that term for it is so closely associated with the care of preschool children. There are some similarities. However, there are also important differences. Day Centers for the older adult serve a population who have lived many years determining their own life's choices. They continue to desire self-determination. They are experienced individuals, eager to share the resources of their life's learnings with others.

Day Centers for older adults are different from Senior Drop-In Centers. The population served at Day Centers is more frail. Program planning therefore, reflects a thorough concern for the participant's well-being. That necessitates an individualized care plan with specific goals including regular health monitoring. It may assume responsibility to remind the participants regarding necessary medications during the day. It planfully involves the participant in activities that will encourage rehabilitation and maintenance.

A typical day for older adults in a Day Center reveals the vital components of its concept. The majority of participants are transported from their homes to the Center by staff. Transportation is provided in mini-buses equipped for wheelchair participants. Upon arriving at the Center, a warm greeting by staff welcomes the participant. The morning is filled with a warm cup of coffee, perhaps discussing the morning newspaper, and a wide variety of activities and exercises which enhance the individual's sense of self-esteem as well as encourage socialization.

After a nutritious noon meal planned for the individual's dietary needs, the afternoon is filled with a brief rest and then a variety of education and entertainment activities. At the end of a full day, participants ride with their friends in the mini-bus to places of residence. The total day's experience intends to meet the needs of the whole individual: physical, social, emotional and spiritual.

## FEASIBILITY: DISCOVERY AND DECISION

The partnership between Lutheran Social Services of Illinois (LSSI) and a local Lutheran parish serves as a working demonstration of adding strength to strength in initiating adult Day Centers. The Social Ministry Committee of the parish, through a process of planning and goal setting, had made a commitment to initiate a major involvement in meeting a high priority community need. The Administrator of the local office of LSSI was invited to be a consultant with the committee. The LSSI Administrator presented three priority options for consideration based on the agency's involvement in the community, an awareness of needs assessment studies, and an awareness of the goals of the parish and its resources. Using the collective knowledge of the Committee about the community's needs and the parish resources, the Committee elected to target the need for Day Centers for the impaired older adult after deliberate and careful consideration.

Following selection of the Day Center concept, the Committee implemented a feasibility study process to determine how such a program could be initiated in the community. Using the knowledge, contacts and resources of both the parish and the agency, considerable background information was assembled about the needs of impaired older adults, the service components of Day Centers, management and fiscal aspects as well as research on the effectiveness of such programs. Selections from the material were copied and shared with the Committee for study and reflection.

The locations of existing Day Centers in Illinois were identified and plans made by committee members and agency staff to visit several of them individually. A majority of the Committee made a group visit to one of the earliest established Day Centers in Illinois (thus having the longest history of operational experience) which also was located in a Lutheran parish. This visit proved most helpful from an informational perspective, but the greatest impact was from the emotional commitment it generated in each person and a consensus of determination to see a similar program initiated locally.

The Committee set aside sufficient funds to enable the LSSI Administrator to attend a week of specialized training at the Gerontological Institute of the University of Michigan specifically focused on the operations of Day Centers. With this professional training, the Administrator was able to provide qualitative consultation to the Committee in its planning.

Using the knowledge and contacts of both the committee members and agency staff, funding resources were explored which included the Illinois Department of Aging, the Area Agency on Aging, the United Way, and local foundations.

The feasibility study phase was a joint effort, with strong involvement of the associate pastor and the Committee Chair, in taking initiatives for implementation. The knowledge, contacts, and resources of the parish joined with those of the agency, gave a breadth, depth, and quality to the study that neither could have accomplished alone.

## NEGOTIATIONS: EDUCATION AND COMMITMENT

When a parish committee or task force of community people identified the need for a Day Center, the search for an appropriate location began. Upon looking for a site, the task force met with local ministerial groups. As far as possible, pastors were invited to visit already existing Day Centers. The need was shared for a parish which would be willing to offer the use of space for a Day Center. Because of the newness of such programs much interpretation is helpful at this point.

A variety of means may be available in educating the prospective parish regarding a Day Center. A temple talk at worship, a discussion with a parish council and/or appropriate committees, a presentation at parish organizational programs, or a combination of the above are all useful. After the willingness to explore the partnership is discovered, it is necessary to negotiate with parish leaders regarding specific needs for the program.

Church building needs include: handicap accessibility, restrooms able to accommodate wheelchairs, a kitchen area, and a bright, large room (approximately 1500 square feet for 20 participants). Before contracting with the parish, it is necessary to explore fire and safety regulations to determine what is required to meet codes. Experience suggests that negotiating these details takes considerable time and frequent meetings. There often is some concern by members of the parish regarding there remaining sufficient space to retain full parish activities. When leaders see a Day Center as an opportunity for expanding the parish's mission in the community, it is a growing time for all members.

It is helpful to engage an attorney to formalize the agreement with the parish into a legal contract. It is often possible to find those services in the community at no cost. The contract becomes a tool for evaluation of the relationship on an annual basis.

## CARE AND FEEDING:
## PROGRAM AND PARISH ADVANTAGES

Perhaps the least concrete, but most pervasive impact of locating a Day Center in the facilities of the parish is to put the sign of the cross over it . . . . both literally and figuratively. The parish context continuously reminds staff of theological principles and values that inform program services and management. Values such as the dignity and worth of the individual, forgiveness and acceptance, personal giving and caring as well as reminders of the spiritual dimension and ultimate concern such as death and the grief process—all these enhance the character and quality of the program.

The Day Center includes regularly scheduled dialogue with pastors. Being located in a church provides an opportunity for program participants who may choose to attend worship service in the chapel setting which is particularly meaningful to persons who are usually homebound.

The partnership with the parish members gives the staff of the Day Center a readily available and willing group of community citizens to educate about the needs of older adults and the capabilities of a Day Center. These church members then become ambassadors to the community for making the program known, interpreting the services of the program, and opening doors to speak to other groups in the community. This is particularly helpful since Day Centers are a largely unknown concept and thus need considerable explanation to the community. Also, many older adults' first response is one of resistance and misunderstanding about Day Centers fearing that it is the first step on a quick path to being placed into a nursing home. The parish members are often able to handle these concerns in the context of a personal relationship, the most effective context. Thus they become a major source of referrals to the program. Of course, the knowledge pastors have of the program and the many family situations to which they provide pastoral ministry make them another ready source of referrals.

The parish partnership provides the Day Center with a variety of human resources. Knowing the philosophy and purpose of the program, members are able to identify qualified candidates for staff positions who also possess a spirit of caring and dedication that provide the "extras" of the program.

Financial resources for most Day Centers are not adequate to provide all the personnel resources needed for a quality program. The partnership is particularly helpful in identifying, recruiting, and sustaining excellent volunteers to assist in the program. The few paid staff positions can never contain the wide range of personal interests and skills that can be effectively utilized in the program. Volunteers with a wide variety of talents are always in use.

The development and maintenance of a strong advisory board is made much easier because of the parish/agency partnership. With the assistance of the pastor and social ministry committee, parish and community persons are identified who would bring to the board the necessary commitment and mix of skills. Since these parish leaders also, in many cases, hold leadership positions in the community, the process of successfully recruiting board members is much easier. With top community leadership, it is possible to access financial support.

Through the social ministry committee, the parish membership is easily accessed for assistance with special needs that surface in the program. If an equipment or supply item is needed that could not be fit into the fiscal limitations, individual members or groups within the church often respond quite readily with the needed item. Particularly helpful are special arrangements that only "connections" make possible, such as locating a river front cabin for a picnic and fishing expedition for Day Center participants.

The partnership provides direct financial assistance to the program as well. Parish groups may designate funds from a particular event for the Day Center. Members trying to identify a beneficiary for memorial funds or bequests are sometimes steered to the program.

The location of the program in church facilities provides large and diverse space options. Space not regularly used by the Day Center can be used on a planned basis for meeting with family members, other social service agency staff, as well as space for special events for the participants or the community at large.

The parish also provides an independent source of evaluation and can validate the program with funding sources and the general community. The program staff provides quarterly reports to the pastors and social ministry committee as a way of keeping the parish informed, as well as providing an opportunity for constructive feedback.

The partnership is not one way, however. The location of the Day Center in the church facilities offers some advantages to the parish. Most parishes struggle with the wise stewardship of facilities that are often used for limited periods of time during the week. With an appropriate design and mutual planning, the Day Center makes use of space five days a week which can also be used during evenings and weekends for other events. This multiple use not only makes for good stewardship, but also creates the opportunity for those using the space to become acquainted with the Day Center. Invariably, someone will ask a question about the room's use, creating the opportunity to increase awareness of the needs of older adults.

With the involvement of the pastor and social ministry committee, as well as the high visibility through use of space in the church, parish members have a readiness to be educated about older adults and their needs. Program staff, as well as other resources, make presentations in forums and as speakers to parish groups. The result may be an increase in the parish's investment in other services to an aging population.

With the Day Center located in the church, the staff, pastor and members serve as a ready resource for information and consultation.

Although the intent of locating the program in the church building is not evangelism, yet its location there presents the sign of the cross to all who come to the program as participant or on other business. The partnership is a concrete demonstration of faith made alive in word and deed.

## SERVICE NETWORKING: DAY CENTER AND COMMUNITY

Serving the frail older population through Day Centers often brings the awareness of the broad scope of needs. It is imperative that staff and parish acquaint themselves with other community-based home services, such as home health care, transportation services, chore housekeeping, etc. Many states now fund such community-based services as alternatives to institutionalization. Also provided are agencies which assess an individual's specific needs and facilitate appropriate referrals.

A Day Center staff cannot perform all of the services helpful to such a client population. Therefore, knowledge of those services in the community and a sound professional relationship with them is important.

# Share-A-Home:
# A Service to Elders

Sandra E. Pranschke

**ABSTRACT.** The Share-A-Home Program operated by Lutheran Social Service of Minnesota was designed to keep senior citizens living in their own homes by finding live-in companions who were willing to help with chores and provide security and companionship in return for an inexpensive place to live. This paper describes the three years of operation of the program from September 1980 to March 1983. During the first three years of operation, the program experienced considerable growth in: (a) demand for service; (b) number of matches made; and (c) number of matches in force each month. In addition, the cost of the program during this time decreased. Interviews with elderly residents in the program revealed that most felt more secure, experienced more companionship, had less trouble taking care of their homes, and were more satisfied with their lives since entering the program. Program participants expressed strong approval of the actions of the Lutheran Social Service staff in arranging their matches. It was concluded that Social Service agency was successful in implementing a program which meets the needs of the elderly by allowing them to remain in their homes and maintain an independent life style.

Share-A-Home is a current program of Lutheran Social Service of Minnesota (LSS) which enables senior citizens to remain in their own homes and avoid unnecessary institutionalization. Younger adults are placed in the homes of elders to provide chore services, companionship, security, and income. Secondary benefits are low-cost housing for young persons and relationships that narrow "generation gaps" between young and old.

Share-A-Home was initiated in 1980 as an innovative response to needs of older persons. Those needs have been most recently reaffirmed by a Minneapolis Citizens League report (1984) that de-

---

Sandra E. Pranschke is with Lutheran Social Service of Minnesota.

scribes excessive institutionalization of senior citizens in Minnesota. Principally supported by a grant from a private foundation and church derived funding, the program concept has been successfully demonstrated and continuously refined. A thorough professional evaluation has been performed.

## OUTREACH

Making the program known and registering elders in the program, have not been problems. The response to the program has been tremendous, particularly by elders and their families. In 1983, 1,528 new telephone contacts were made, and 426 potential live-ins and senior citizens were registered.

In the future, additional emphasis will be given to recruiting adult live-ins. Not only will contacts with local secondary educational institutions be intensified to secure referrals of students, but LSS will experiment more with other categories of potential live-ins (adults in entry-level jobs or low-salaried fields, single adults, other elders, etc.)

Program staff produced and broadly distributed brochures describing the program and inviting referrals to appropriate community agencies. Staff appeared before 12 local groups in 1983 to describe the program, and will continue to respond to such invitations. Share-A-Home is represented at all major resource fairs in Minneapolis for senior citizens. By far the largest single source of referrals for residents has been other human service agencies. For example, many followed the advice of hospital staff and contacted the program during recovery from an illness. The second largest source was word of mouth. This would seem to indicate that the publicity work done by the program staff has resulted in considerable visibility in both the human services community and the general public.

Share-A-Home has also attracted considerable media attention. Major feature stories have appeared in the *Minneapolis Tribune* and the *St. Paul Pioneer Press*. Additional coverage has been provided by area shopping newspapers and even one national newspaper, *Grit*. Articles describing the program have appeared in *The Lutheran Standard*, the professional journal, *Geriatric Residential Care*, and most recently, in the *College Housing News*. A record number of inquiries followed feature stories in Twin Cities' papers.

Share-A-Home has also been featured on three local television programs. Volunteer opportunities are advertised through the United Way's Voluntary Action Center, Volunteer Market Place, RSVP, and the LSS Auxiliary.

## PROBLEMS OF ELDERS

The specific problems faced by elders and the extent of their needs were first described in a Housing Position Paper of the Metropolitan Council's Aging Program. Of the estimated 180,000 senior citizens living in the Twin Cities area in 1980, about 63,000 were thought to be capable of semi-independent living, that is, capable of maintaining their own home *only* if some assistance was provided. These are the "frail elderly," 75 years of age and older, who are isolated by the death of their spouse and by chronic health problems. While most prefer to maintain independent living in their own homes, they are confronted by strenuous chores, fear of being criminally victimized, loneliness, and rising utility costs. Since only a fraction of these elders was thought to be receiving housekeeping aids or in-home nursing care, "shared housing" was proposed as a possible solution to this problem. A special Task Force on Alternative Housing for the Elderly, at LSS, then developed the concept of Share-A-Home. Funds were sought and received from a private foundation to begin the program in April 1980, and the program has since been successfully implemented.

When Share-A-Home and other services are not available to support elderly in their homes, the elders are forced to accept placement in expensive residential programs. The consequence of these unnecessary placements are the loss of personal independence valued by the elders and great financial expense incurred by elders and society. A recent Citizens League report documents the overuse of nursing homes for care of senior citizens in Minnesota and recommends the expansion of alternatives to such institutionalization. In 1983, the Metropolitan Council publicly recommended expansion of the LSS Share-A-Home Program as an innovative alternative.

While the inability of senior citizens to live independently is the principal problem addressed by Share-A-Home, two other significant community problems are also impacted. First, young adults, particularly students and those in entry level employment, do not have the financial resources to obtain market rate rental housing. Through Share-A-Home matches with elders, younger adults receive housing and other benefits at little or no cash expense. Secondly, changes in American family life-styles are opening "generation gaps" between young and old persons. Many Americans are growing up without significant exposure to older persons, and older persons often feel alienated by youth. Intergenerational experiences, like those created through Share-A-Home matches, challenge false stereotypes of older persons, reduce alienation between generations, and build healthy understanding and acceptance of the normal aging process.

## SERVICES OF SHARE-A-HOME

There are a number of approaches to "shared housing" programs. Each has different objectives and utilizes different methods. One approach only provides the potential live-in with a list of residents who have expressed an interest in taking in boarders. The responsibility for making a suitable match rests with the program participants and usually involves no more than one interview with the program staff.

The LSS Share-A-Home Program, however, has chosen to use a more responsible "counseling" approach in making matches. The "counseling" approach requires considerable time from volunteers or paid staff. A typical match involves about 17 phone calls, at least one interview at the LSS office and usually two or more home visits. The Share-A-Home staff believe that this investment of time is important to insure the safety of residents and to improve the chances of making enduring matches.

Ordinarily, the matching process starts with an inquiry from the older person, a friend, a relative, or a social worker. A visit is made to the elder's home for an interview with the client. An assessment is made of the client's attitudes, expectations, needs, and life-style. Potential live-ins are oriented to the program in group sessions, are interviewed, submit background information, and provide references. Matches are made on the basis of compatible needs and expectations. After a few days' time for thinking it over, the parties are asked to sign a written agreement for the match outlining services to be provided, accommodations available, and any financial terms. Periodic contacts are made after the match is completed to identify and resolve emergent problems.

To help support services and to increase client commitment to making matches work, LSS charges a $10 registration fee and a $100 fee from both parties when a match is made. This fee is waived if it seems beyond the means of a participant; volunteer service is also accepted as an alternative to payment.

In addition to providing services directly to clients in the local community, Share-A-Home is a model program that can be replicated elsewhere in the metro area, the state, and the nation. The program has received national attention in the media. College housing bureau directors have inquired about how to make use of shared housing for their students. Other agencies, church groups, and charitable organizations have requested advice in setting up their own programs.

The LSS staff has also been instrumental in the formation of a network of shared housing programs in the state. Lutheran Social Service hosted the first meeting of shared housing program operators in August, 1982. It was attended by representatives of nine programs from Minnesota and Wisconsin. Conferences have been held in subsequent years and in May 1983, the Minnesota Coalition on Home Sharing was founded. This represents the beginning of a cooperative network for sharing information and providing mutual assistance in finding suitable housing for live-ins and residents.

## EVALUATION OF SHARE-A-HOME

Share-A-Home was originally funded by a private foundation in 1980 as a significant new demonstration effort. The foundation provided separate funding to support professional evaluation and information dissemination activities. A team of licensed consulting psychologists was contracted for evaluation services. Extensive evaluation reports were produced at the end of the first, second and third program years.

Share-A-Home is clearly a cost-effective approach to meeting needs of elders; when compared with other services that help sustain elders, Share-A-Home costs per day in 1983 were very reasonable:

Share-A-Home                                    $ 3.90

Personal care help in home                       26.80

Nursing care in home                             29.80

Homemaking and housekeeping                      67.50

Intermediate care in residential facility        48.92

Since that report was completed, Share-A-Home has modified the program and made it more effective and efficient. Statistical information has been collected to monitor program accomplishments. Progress has been made in increasing the average length of matches, reducing the number of matches terminating in the first 30 days, and reducing the per diem cost of the service.

Share-A-Home as a model is adaptable to the parish level or perhaps more logically to a consortium of Churches.

Volunteers might be recruited from existing groups such as Social Ministry Committees, friendly visiting groups, or perhaps visitation staff might be able to take on the added responsibility. Their tasks would be to refer and interview elders, perhaps assist in the matching process, and to provide monitoring of the match. Participants in the program have provided these services for the LSS program. In the Lutheran Social Service of Minnesota Metro West Office, paid and volunteer staff work cooperatively as a team to provide service to the elders of Minneapolis and St. Paul.

## REFERENCES

Anderson, Nancy N., Patten, Sharon K., and Greenberg, Jay N. *A comparison of home care and nursing home care for older persons in Minnesota.* The Administration on Aging, U.S. Department of Health and Human Services (No. 90-A-682). 1980 University of Minnesota.

*National directory of shared housing programs.* Shared Housing Resource Center, Inc., 6344 Greene Street, Philadelphia, Pennsylvania 19144.

Staples, Emily Anne, Chair of Institutionalization Committee. *Meeting the crisis in institutional care: Toward better choices, financing and results.* Minneapolis Minnesota Citizens League, April, 1984.

Table 1

A Possible Budget

| | |
|---|---:|
| Full-time social worker (salary, benefits, taxes) | $25,197.00 |
| Clerical services (.20 FTE) | 4,287.00 |
| Occupancy ($200/mo.) | 3,200.00 |
| Telephone | 800.00 |
| Staff transportation | 1,867.00 |
| Office supplies | 133.00 |
| Training and consultation | 6,240.00 |
| Conferences and workshops | 200.00 |
| Office equipment | 67.00 |
| Hospitality and recruitment | 267.00 |
| Administrative support | 6,333.00 |

# Legal Guardianship for the Elderly: A Volunteer Model

Albert W. Keyser

**ABSTRACT.** The Volunteer Guardianship Program of Lutheran Ministries of Florida serves as a guardian of last resort for adults who have been adjudicated incompetent by the court and for whom no other guardian is available. The need for such a ministry is especially great in Florida's Suncoast Area where a great many people are over age 75 and separated from family support systems. While Florida statutes make no provisions for public guardianship, Florida law does allow nonprofit corporations to be appointed guardian of person and/or property. Under this statute, Lutheran Ministries of Florida serves as the court appointed guardian for incompetent persons. It uses a teamwork approach involving professional staff and trained volunteers to assure that the needs of the ward are met.

## INTRODUCTION

A guardian is the court-appointed representative for an individual who has been ruled mentally or physically incompetent. In Florida, a guardian of person must be appointed and a guardian of property may be appointed. The guardian of person is responsible for the personal care of the ward, to see that an appropriate place of residence is secured, to see that medical and psychiatric care is provided, and to abide by the ward's preferences as is practical. The guardian of property is responsible for the wise management of the ward's assets. The guardian of person and property each provide an annual accounting to the court. LMF usually serves as both.

As an advocate for the ward, a primary guideline for the guardian is the Prudent Person Rule; namely, to act on behalf of the ward in a prudent manner. Thus, serving as legal guardian is a comprehensive responsibility in that the guardian is responsible for all aspects of the ward's well being.

---

Albert W. Keyser is with Lutheran Ministries of Florida, Suncoast Area.

*41*

The purpose of the Volunteer Guardianship Program in Florida is to serve as a guardian of last resort for adults who have been adjudicated incompetent by the court and for whom no other guardian is available. In this program, Lutheran Ministries of Florida, a nonprofit corporation, is appointed guardian and uses a teamwork model involving professional staff and trained volunteers to carry out the duties of the guardianship.

## ASSESSMENT OF NEED

The need for such a ministry is especially great on Florida's Suncoast where 36% of the population are over age 60 and 12% are over age 75. Eight percent (8%) fall below the poverty level and many more hover just above it. A majority of these people have no family in the state of Florida since they had left family behind when they retired to Florida.

Further, Pinellas County, Florida alone has over 60 of Florida's 160+ nursing homes. A survey of these homes by a Lutheran Ministries of Florida volunteer revealed that up to 75% of the residents in some nursing homes had no regular visitation from anyone.

The isolation and poverty of these elders make many susceptible to abuse, exploitation and neglect as the multiple losses that often accompany old age make them less and less capable of caring for themselves and managing their affairs.

While Pinellas County has a strong community of professional guardians who serve incompetent persons able to pay guardianship fees and many indigent wards as well, most of the incompetent, isolated, elderly poor have gone without this care.

The Volunteer Guardianship Program has addressed this need for guardians of last resort and is seeking to strengthen its funding base so that it may better address the need.

## CORPORATE GUARDIANSHIP

In Florida, a nonprofit corporation may become the court appointed guardian of person and/or property. Lutheran Ministries of Florida (LMF) is, therefore, the legally appointed guardian. Staff and volunteers act on behalf of LMF.

Responsibility assumed by LMF is important in securing and maintaining volunteers since the volunteers need not assume the ultimate legal liability for the ward. Under the corporate guardianship, volunteers have the support and partnership of professional staff and other volunteers. In addition, an added advantage is that when a volunteer wants to resign or take a break for vacation, no legal action is necessary to change personnel, because the guardian remains LMF.

## CLIENTS SERVED

The people served by the Volunteer Guardianship Program have been adjudicated incompetent by the court. This may have come about due to increasing impairments, deteriorating physical or mental health, uncooperativeness with helping efforts, financial vulnerability or legal difficulties.

While most LMF wards are over age 60, some are younger adults who suffer from mental retardation or deterioration due to alcoholism or mental illness.

When LMF is appointed guardian, alternatives have already been explored by The Florida Department of Health and Rehabilitative Services or hospital social services. The incompetency action is taken because community resources offer no alternative that would afford adequate care. In the continuum of care for the elderly, guardianship is the service required when Meals on Wheels, homemaker, chore and visiting nurses can no longer make independent or minimally supported living possible. The client must be placed in the care of another.

## REFERRAL NETWORK

Referrals to the Volunteer Guardianship Program come from attorneys, the court, the Department of Health and Rehabilitative Services, hospitals, churches and families.

To accept a referral, casework must have been done to explore alternatives to guardianship, the attorney of record secured, the incompetency petition filed with the court; and in most cases, alternative guardian possibilities exhausted.

## VOLUNTEER APPOINTMENT AND EXPECTATIONS

Upon acceptance of a referral, the Guardianship Coordinator and Volunteer Coordinator confer as to the needs of the guardianship, and the volunteer best suited to working with that particular client is chosen. Considerations include the situation and needs of the ward, skills and health of the volunteer, age and interest similarities, geographical proximity, time flexibility, and religious background and sensitivities.

A pre-screened volunteer is selected and offered the opportunity to become involved based on preliminary information about the prospective ward. The volunteer attends the incompetency hearing and then initiates the care of the ward with the Guardianship Coordinator.

Duties of volunteer guardians include, participation in an initial basic training, participation in a bi-monthly case conference with staff and other volunteers, at least bi-weekly visits to the ward, attention to the needs of the ward, active communication with the staff regarding the condition and needs of the ward and regular contact with family members.

### SERVING AS GUARDIAN

Following LMF's appointment, the volunteer is provided credentials by LMF and proceeds to initiate care under staff supervision.

In order to prepare a comprehensive plan to provide for a ward's care, the volunteer and staff review all information leading to the ward's adjudication. They also obtain and review any other medical and social work records. Interviews with the ward as well as family or friends help provide a thorough understanding of the ward's history, condition and current requirements.

An individual guardianship plan is developed for the ward within two weeks of appointment by the court. The plan includes: (a) a determination of the most appropriate placement; (b) necessary services anticipated for at least six months; (c) a goal for the ward's functioning level to be evaluated in six months; and (d) plans for restoration of competency if possible.

Volunteers secure, for safekeeping, all relevant legal documents and credit cards in the possession of the ward. These may include birth certificates, social security cards, voter identification cards, driver licenses, marriage licenses, insurance policies, deeds, bank information, etc. The volunteer also works with the ward's bank to place his assets under guardianship. Within 60 days of appointment, an inventory of all assets must be filed with the court. The volunteer, with a witness present, records all of the ward's possessions. A copy is sent by LMF to the attorney of record.

Paid staff include the Guardianship Coordinator, Assistant Coordinator, Volunteer Coordinator, Secretary and two part time Clerks. The Guardianship Coordinator is responsible for management of the program, general oversight of all case management, and management of all guardian of person issues. The Assistant Coordinator is responsible for managing guardian of property concerns. In addition to secretarial work, the Secretary supervises banking for wards and assists in many areas relating to attorneys and care providers. The Volunteer Coordinator recruits, trains, and supports volunteers, and seeks substitute volunteers to provide transportation, visitation and other services when the primary volunteer is unavailable.

Professional staff have ultimate responsibility to assure that each ward receives appropriate and adequate services. Staff are responsible for volunteer recruitment and training, case management, supervision and overall program management. Staff provide professional support to volunteers, prepare individual guardianship plans, locate community resources necessary for the ward. The Guardianship Coordinator or his designee is on call 24 hours per day.

## EVALUATION

Since clients are all legally incompetent persons, evaluation of the program must use more than client feedback. Hence, a satisfaction survey is used annually with attorneys, social workers, nursing and boarding home personnel, and medical and psychiatric personnel.

A multi-disciplinary Guardianship Advisory Committee meets quarterly to discuss policy, fund raising and other concerns.

## FUNDING

Permanent funding remains in question. The program was initiated with seed money from a major Lutheran church. Part time service delivery was initiated with two years of funding from another church body. With part time and volunteer staff only, the program grew to serve 47 people.

LMF was chosen to serve as a Public Guardianship Pilot Project for the Office of the State Courts Administrator in 1983. This allowed hiring of a full time Guardianship Coordinator and further growth of the program. The Pilot Project expired after 12 months and no new funding resulted.

Older American's Act funds from the Area Agency on Aging were secured in July 1983. This allowed maintenance of the service initiated by the Pilot Project. These funds expired December 31, 1984.

Since, funds have come from Pinellas County, The Florida Bar, The City of St. Petersburg, The Pinellas County Community Foundation, Guardianship fees for non-indigent wards, churches, and individuals. A variety of other sources are approached to complete the needed $100,000 to serve 100 wards.

Clearly, a permanent source of major funding is needed.

## REPLICATION

In states where nonprofit corporations may serve as a legal guardian, the Volunteer Guardianship Program is a way that congregations or agencies can serve their own members and/or the community at large.

In an agency, professional staff can supervise volunteers very effectively. In a congregation, the pastor and a team of lay people can carry out all guardianship responsibilities and retain care of the person within the church.

# Congregate Housing as an Alternative to Institutionalization for the Frail Elderly

Hans-J.R. Irmer

**ABSTRACT.** This paper summarizes a fellowship project completed in 1982 at the Hebrew Rehabilitation Center for Aged (The Center) in Boston, Massachusetts. The fellowship was jointly funded by a W. K. Kellogg Fellowship granted by the Hospital Research and Educational Trust, Chicago, Illinois and by The Center. At its completion, the project proposed a concept of supportive elderly congregate housing designed for persons not only requiring assistance with such vital activities as eating, dressing, and grooming but also lacking adequate support from family and friends. Confronted by gaps in our health and social service systems, these elderly often struggle with whether to remain in independent living arrangements without adequate coping mechanisms or to enter long term care institutions which may provide more services than are needed. Four components of this housing are discussed: A Tenant Profile describing potential residents; recommendations for environmental features; services to be provided; and financial resources. Data was drawn from a variety of sources including applicants and residents of a large long-term care facility and tenants of a large housing project. Ten site visits were made and research findings were reviewed. Interdisciplinary committees evaluated the data to develop goals, criteria, and recommendations. With refined selection techniques and good management, this housing should be cost effective and complement emerging life-styles of Americans. It should also be highly beneficial for a segment of the elderly who might otherwise reside, unnecessarily, in nursing homes.

Demographic studies repeatedly describe an elderly population that is growing dramatically. Since the incidence of morbidity is a positive function of age, these statistics also predict increasing demands for healthcare and support services.

The author is currently serving as the Pastor/Administrator of the Martin Luther Nursing Home, Inc., Clinton, New York.

47

According to the Federal Council on Aging (1982), the percentage of elderly needing assistance with the personal activities of daily living (e.g., bathing, eating, dressing, toileting, and grooming) increases at least five-fold between the ages 65 and 85.[1] For the vast majority of these elderly, family members and friends provide needed services. However, for a sizeable minority, the informal support network is absent or otherwise unable to meet critical needs. These elderly persons must look elsewhere for support and are frequently confronted by a gap in the health care delivery system. They must choose between remaining in independent living arrangements with inadequate coping mechanisms, or entering long-term care institutions which provide more services than may be needed. As a result, many enter nursing homes to receive extensive assistance with the activities of daily living; but *not* because they require the specialized care that can only be provided by the licensed personnel in these homes.

Researchers state that between 10 and 30 percent[2] of residents in nursing homes could function in less supportive environments. Unfortunately, in light of their continuous and extensive needs many of these persons find home care services to be inadequate or excessively expensive. On the other hand, entry into nursing homes involves several high price tags. For example, researchers indicate that, once elderly persons enter institutions they are harder to deinstitutionalize than other population sub-groups. Furthermore, since people frequently assume the roles suggested by their environment, institutional populations often look and act sicker than similar persons in less restricted environments.

Supportive elderly housing appears to be a highly appropriate solution for responding to the needs of this population and improving quality of life. Housing responsive to functional needs can compensate for or alleviate a variety of limitations; and selected services can make it possible for some elderly people now entering nursing homes to continue to live in the community. Those who may be quite frail, yet motivated and capable of living independently with proper supports, could thus lead more meaningful lives than would be otherwise possible. Moreover, supportive housing could also facilitate better use of limited healthcare resources while they are being strained by current levels of demand. Given good management and careful selection procedures, this housing would prove to be cost-effective and highly beneficial for a significant number of elderly people.

Looking to the future, it also seems that upcoming generations of Americans striving to maintain independent lifestyles will avoid entering institutions for as long as possible. Again, supportive housing would be a sensitive and meaningful response to this rapidly increasing elderly populace.

## OBJECTIVES

As suggested above, the primary goal of this project was to assemble a plan for housing to accommodate elderly persons who frequently have no option other than institutionalization. Pursuit of this goal included two related objectives: (1) careful definition of the population to be served by such specialized housing and (2) development of a cost-effective plan for implementing and maintaining it. As a measurable goal, the primary indicator of success would be a commitment by The Center to construct housing based on the findings and recommendations of this project.

## METHODOLOGY

A variety of resources and numerous personnel assisted with compiling plans for this concept of specialized housing. These included: an Advisory Council; interdisciplinary staff committees; site visits of operating housing projects; and a review of the literature. Data were also collected to analyze the needs of: current nursing home residents and applicants, current and former tenants of a large elderly housing complex, and disabled elderly clients being served in their homes by community agencies.

The advisory council guided the overall progress of the project and served as the primary resource for identifying potential avenues of funding. Because of the magnitude of the task and due to findings that group-based methodologies often result in better quality decisions, the interdisciplinary committees developed recommendations for the major components of the project: The Tenant Profile, Environmental Features, and Services.

## RESULTS

In drafting recommendations for this model of housing, five written documents were compiled. Although these documents are found in their entirety in the Final Report of the project, highlights are summarized below.

*Statement of Goals*

With good planning, careful management and effective selection procedures, this housing would: (1) Make it possible for elderly persons with unmet functional needs to avoid or significantly delay entering a long-term care facility; (2) Be cost-effective, while providing a good quality of life for a mix of well and frail elderly persons; (3) Grant priority status for accepting frail elderly persons who are in institutions or at high risk of entering institutions; (4) Offer services designed to achieve the delicate balance between meeting critical needs and maintaining independence without discouraging the ongoing assistance of informal support systems; and (5) Become well integrated into the community and its programs for the elderly.

*Tenant Profile*

To develop a Tenant Profile that would be successful in fulfilling the vision and goals for this housing, data from residents at The Center and approved applicants on the Waiting List were analyzed to understand why elderly are either entering or already residing in nursing homes. In addition, representatives of community agencies serving frail elderly citizens were interviewed and reports of site visits to housing projects were reviewed. Research findings were also reviewed to understand these unmet needs more fully. Particularly informative were studies by The Center's Department of Social Gerontological Research which emphasized the crucial role of the informal support systems. For example, with resilient support systems many severely handicapped elderly can live good quality lives without being institutionalized. In contrast, elderly persons with decidedly fewer impairments are highly vulnerable to institutionalization if informal supports are absent or limited.

Given all this data, it was possible to identify the functional unmet needs that precede the application of elderly persons to long-term care facilities. Concurrently, it was also determined which of these unmet functional deficits could reasonably be met by the specialized housing and preclude the necessity of placement in a nursing home or similar setting.

The applicants who would qualify as "frail elderly tenants requiring special services" would demonstrate critical unmet functional needs to justify admission into a long-term care facility. In other words, the assistance available from their support system and community resources is not adequate for them to live at an acceptable level. These tenants may have ongoing medical problems, but their conditions will be stable and have a high likelihood of being managed by community resources.

While this housing is intended to enable tenants to fulfill critical unmet needs, it is also important that tenants be able to achieve a good quality of life. Consequently, certain capabilities were recommended as being required. For example, all prospective tenants should possess: (1) a level of mentality sufficient for pursuing an independent life-style; (2) a modicum of mobility skills enabling utilization of an apartment environment; and (3) the motivation to live as independently as possible.

To test the utility of the Tenant Profile, a random sampling of more than 250 approved applicants on The Center's Waiting List was analyzed. In addition, a similar random sampling of current residents was conducted. It was found that approximately 25 to 30 percent of both samples would be suitable applicants for this housing, which is consistent with published estimates of nursing home residents and applicants who could live in less supportive settings.

## Environmental Recommendations

A detailed set of recommendations for the environmental features was assembled according to: general environment and common areas; individual apartments; safety and security; and site selection. In developing recommendations, it was determined that the environment should: (1) encourage tenants to be as independent as is feasible and minimize the need for assistance; (2) be highly marketable (homelike) to both frail and well elderly applicants; (3) facilitate access and utilization of the grounds; (4) promote contacts with families and friends; (5) promote safety and security; (6) facilitate access to the community as well as the community's access to the project (for visiting, volunteering, etc.); (7) facilitate delivery of services; and (8) be financially reasonable and cost-effective.

## Service Recommendations

In order to accomodate a significant number of frail elderly, an inclusive service package was recommended. Again, the formula-

tion of recommendations began with the development of goals, i.e.:
(1) The services will facilitate tenants' independence without creating unnecessary dependence; therefore, the minimum number of services should be provided in order to assist and encourage tenants to live as independently as possible. (2) The service package will be financially feasible for tenants, management and third party payers. (To accomplish this, unlicensed personnel would be employed as primary service providers, the volunteer efforts of tenants and community residents would be promoted and, insofar as possible, the service package will augment—not replace—the informal support system.) (3) The service package will be organized so as to preclude licensure as a health care facility. (4) The administration of the service package will recognize community resources and develop alliances with these providers. (5) The services will be delivered in a manner conducive to a homelike atmosphere.

Generally, the services would provide assistance with the personal and instrumental activities of daily living. Examples include: (1) limited daily assistance with dressing, bathing, grooming, etc.; (2) two meals daily; (3) housekeeping assistance; (4) transfer and transportation services; (5) modest structural adaptations within individual apartments; and (6) extensive information and referral services to assist with shopping, healthcare, finances, etc.

The recommendations also addressed some of the unique concerns of this setting, such as: the decision to provide specific services or enter into contracts with outside agencies; the maintenance of the informal support network; the use of volunteers; the degree of flexibility in the service package to accommodate fluctuations of needs; and the need to establish service parameters in order to maintain the desired tenant profile.

### Financing Options

Given the decision to implement this housing concept, it would be necessary to acquire financial resources for the four major components of the housing, i.e., construction, rental assistance, service package assistance, and research. Various financing options were identified and briefly discussed. Although financing is dependent upon the political and economic milieu, the options recorded in the Final Report should be helpful in identifying potential financing mechanisms.

## Research

With the delivery of services to the elderly affecting so many sectors, this housing would have widespread significance. To assess and strengthen its impact, it would be helpful to conduct research to measure its success in meeting the goals established, particularly: its effect on the quality of tenants' lives; its ability to help tenants avoid or delay entering institutions; its cost effectiveness; and, its success in reaching members of the target population, that is, elderly persons with critical unmet needs.

## EVALUATION AND USEFULNESS

Throughout the project, the need for this type of housing and its potential benefits were repeatedly reinforced by a wide variety of professionals dedicated to the care of the elderly.

As indicated, this housing should be significant for a broad spectrum of organizations and individuals: nonprofit organizations that are potential sponsors of elderly housing, as well as long-term care institutions, community hospitals, Medicaid and Medicare, and community social welfare agencies.

The proposed housing should prove beneficial to the healthcare system by reducing expenditures for a segment of the elderly who reside needlessly in nursing homes. Specific efficiencies could be gained by: (1) utilizing unlicensed attendants to provide supportive services; (2) providing only those services necessary for support (thus decreasing the opportunities for services) that can occur in institutional settings; (3) clustering a portion of the elderly currently receiving community services and promoting efficient service delivery; (4) providing a supportive setting for care upon discharge from acute hospitals and thereby shortening hospital stays; (5) augmenting informal support systems to prevent family members from becoming overburdened in their care of an elderly loved one; (6) creating new informal support systems by establishing a mix of frail elderly and well elderly persons in congregate housing; and (7) utilizing volunteer services.

Of course, the primary beneficiaries will be the elderly themselves. In such a setting, those who may be frail, but are motivated and capable of living independently with the proper supports, will be enabled to lead fuller and more meaningful lives than would have been possible otherwise.

Given the Judaeo-Christian ethic of responsibility to the elderly and those in need, agencies and institutions sponsored by the Church have a mandate to provide high quality care and sensitive living environments for the elderly. The Church can make unique and significant contributions by sponsoring, advocating and planning for innovative elderly housing which may respond to needs as yet unmet.

## NOTES

1. U.S. Department of Health and Human Services. *The Need for Long Term Care, Information and Issues: A Chartbook of the Federal Council on the Aging.* Washington, D.C.: Government Printing Office, 1981. (Publication #OHDS 8120704.), p. 31.
2. Gutkin, Claire E. and Morris, John N. *Impairment Levels and Related Service Needs of the Elderly Functionally Impaired in Delaware.* Boston, MA: Hebrew Rehabilitation Center for Aged, May 1981, p. 38.

## REFERENCES

American Association of Homes for the Aging. *Planning housing and services for the elderly: A process guidebook.* Washington, D.C.: American Association of Homes for the Aging, 1977.

"Architectural and transportation barriers compliance board: Minimum guidelines and requirements for accessible design; Final rule." *Federal Register,* 46 (January 16, 1981), pp. 4270-4304.

Donahue, W.T., Thompson, M. McGuire, and Curren, D.J., ed. *Congregate housing for older people: An urgent need, a growing demand.* Washington, D.C.: Government Printing Office, 1977. (Publication #OHD77-20284.)

Morris, John N. and Sherwood, Sylvia. "A program for meeting the needs of nursing home applicants who have intact communication skills" *Long Term Care Demonstration Project, Final Report Appendix.* Minneapolis, MN: Foundation for Health Care Evaluation, 1979.

Sherwood, S., Greer, D.S., Morris, J.N., Mor, V. and Associates, *An alternative in longterm care: The highland heights experiment.* Ballinger Publication Company, Cambridge, Massachusetts, 1981.

Sherwood, Sylvia, Morris, John N. and Gutkin, Claire LE. *Meeting the needs of the impaired elderly: The power and resiliency of the informal support system.* Boston, MA: Hebrew Rehabilitation Center for Aged. November 1981.

U.S. Department of Housing and Urban Development. *Evaluation of the effectiveness of congregate housing for the elderly.* Washington, D.C.: Government Printing Office, 1976. (Publication #HUD-PDR-198-2.)

# Retirement Homes . . . Boom or Bust?

## John R. Steinhaus

**ABSTRACT.** The Church can ill afford to have any of its sponsored retirement homes become embarrassing "failures." This analysis brings into focus some of the pitfalls that can trap the inexperienced. Areas of special concern include: (1) the planning process; (2) the Board of Directors; (3) the financial plans; (4) the marketing plan; and the unique opportunities of (5) church sponsorship. If we learn from each other and share with each other, and if we use the expertise that we have within our Church family, we should be able to grow with the demand, avoid failures, and be successful in every way.

### INTRODUCTION

Many retirement home planners, promoters, and developers are proclaiming the arrival of the retirement home boom. In a recent current periodical,* an article with the title "Poised On The Threshold of a Boom," begins with the sentence, "After an uncertain start, Continuing Care Centers are now poised on the threshold of a boom." This is good news for those of us who are interested or involved in such programs. How unfortunate, unnecessary, and downright embarrassing, however, when our own Church even once in a while gets involved in a *bust*, not a *boom*!

Most experts in the field probably will agree that there is a growing need for our retirement homes. There no doubt will be a boom. But along with the success stories, there is a good chance that there will be a number of sad failures unless we are careful and follow the formula for success. Since we in the church have had both kinds of experiences, it would be well that we not only learn from our experiences, but that we share our insights and expertise so that our future efforts will all be success stories.

---

John R. Steinhaus is President and CEO, California Lutheran Homes, Alhambra, California.

*Nauert, Roger C., "Poised On the Threshold of a Boom," *Contemporary Administrator*, Vol. 7, pp. 45 ff., September, 1984.

Over the past twenty years, California Lutheran Homes has "rescued" three Continuing Care Centers (CCCs) that were either in bankruptcy or headed for it. We have been consultants in a number of other instances. When we diagnose and analyze the pitfalls of retirement home development, the problems become unbelievably involved and complicated. In this review we will try to avoid the temptation to get into the details and touch only on the highlights.

It is interesting how different analysts from different backgrounds tend to stress different problems as being the major cause of trouble. Financial experts emphasize that most failures come from the lack of proper financial planning, pricing, setting of rates, inadequate projections, etc. Administrators notice that bad management causes most of the failures. Social planners tell us that we have misjudged the market or do not understand the needs and wants of the people to be served. Each point of view deserves to be heard. We know that big dollars are involved. We know that only the best kind of management will be able to handle what is becoming increasingly a very complicated business. And we know that understanding the older adult and the lifestyles that they want and need is not nearly as easy as we used to assume. This challenge is no longer for the amateurs. Success in retirement home development is a theological exception; it does not come from "faith alone."

## THE PLANNERS

Nearly all of our problems come from new groups who try to plan a Retirement Home or CCC for the first time. Somehow the idea lingers that all it takes is common sense. The truth is that it is a very specialized task with pitfalls that can fool even the experts. Too often the planners are good-hearted people who are better dreamers than planners. Good plans are the result of disciplined study and require a thorough knowledge of the field. Highlights of the most common pitfalls are summarized below:

### Motivation

Most groups are motivated for some of the right reasons: to serve, to witness, to make life better for older people, and to have a viable business. We need to be careful that it is not to build a monument, build a membership for a nearby congregation, develop a project on land that happens to be available, provide business for friendly contractors or realtors, etc.

## Design of Building and Program

Sometimes our planners do not realize that the home needs to be designed for the long-range demand. There are many kinds of services and programs to consider, and a delicate balance of independent living, residential care, personal care, intermediate care and skilled nursing care. The size of the total project, the types of living units, flexibility, the target resident (couples, singles, the young old, old or old old), the needs, the financial resources, the trends, and location. These are not random options. Only some of them, carefully put together, will add up to a successful venture.

## Consultants

Since the planning phase can make or break the project, it is almost essential that any inexperienced group retain the proper consultants and architects. We cannot take chances on any consultant or architect who does not have the experience and a proven track record.

## THE BOARD OF DIRECTORS

The governing board of a CCC is much more than a group of good people who share their time and talent. Because so many dollars are involved and so many lives are affected, the responsibility (and liability) is profoundly serious.

The volunteer Board of a nonprofit (church-related) CCC is a beautiful example of Christian stewardship. But it also can be a weak link in the organization. If the Board does not have CCC expertise, then it is doubly important that the management staff has the experience and the expertise.

A strange phenomenon seems to happen when outstanding individuals become a nonprofit Board and somehow collectively abandon the business principles that they use in their own business. Some Boards take on a strange ''nonprofit'' mentality suggesting that God is in control of the bottom line and that somehow they can give away more than they take in. It is good to be ''charitable,'' but no one can give away something he does not have. The nonprofit Board can be no less accountable for its stewardship than the businessman who is using his own money. In fact, since most of the money involved is the money of elderly residents, even more accountability is required.

## THE FINANCIAL PLANS

In recent years a number of experts have analyzed the pitfalls of financial planning for CCC's. A group that starts with no "investor capital" is expecting miracles. Of course miracles do happen, but to finance a project 100% is risky, to say the least. It is impossible to overemphasize the need for cautious, careful and sound financial planning.

*Projections* are a required part of every lending program. This author has seen hundreds of projections, but not a single one could be considered as gospel. A conservative, careful, expert projection is only a guess. Something always happens to make it miss. But of course, good projections are necessary; they need to be for at least fifteen years when Accommodation Fees (Entrance Fees, Founders Fees, etc.) are involved, and they need to be updated constantly. But the Board of Directors and the Management team should know how fickle these projections can be.

*Other Financial Pitfalls* seem to be:

1. Actuarial Tables
2. Predicting the age and health conditions of new admissions
3. Establishing adequate but marketable fees
4. Medical costs and how they vary
5. Investment policies (for reserves and special funds)
6. A realistic appraisal of "charity" subsidies.

A special emphasis should be given to the necessity of a long range program of *Endowments* for the CCC. Financial security can rarely come from the nip and tuck battle of operating revenue versus operating expense. If a CCC wants to be truly a nonprofit charitable organization and if it wants stability to weather the surprise storms of unexpected expense, then an Endowment Fund is an absolute necessity. Every church-related organization is a logical nucleus for Endowment growth. It takes special expertise and it may start slowly, but start and grow it must!

## THE BUNDLE OF SERVICES

Can any CCC provide too many services for their residents? It can if the costs are not covered. It can if the services are not those wanted or needed by the residents. It can if those services are subject greatly to control by outside powers i.e., government, inflation, medical community, etc.

There is a temptation for organizations to promise too much in their "Resident Agreements" ("it makes marketing easier"). Fringe benefits, such as transportation, telephone, medical services, bath supplies, extra food, etc., can add up to many dollars. A very marketable solution to the problem seems to be a trend in many successful CCCs these recent years. Options are given on an "a la carte" basis so that people pay for what they get—no more, no less. The extent of medical care is a good case in point. If a small CCC uses the group insurance approach to cover too many medical services, the dollar fluctuations can be extreme either way. If some basic services are offered in the basic bundle of services but major services are "a la carte," the outcome is much more predictable.

The most marketable services today may not be the most marketable tomorrow. It is important to have a flexible bundle of services so that the CCC will always know what the target audience wants and what it is willing to pay.

Present day researchers and today's most successful CCCs are being innovative in the most fascinating ways. New services that are meaningful and productive are being suggested. Needs assessment programs, "work" opportunities, therapeutic activities, life review programs, etc., are not the traditional bundle of services, but they are beginning to change the direction for future CCCs.

## THE MANAGEMENT TEAM

Books, of course, are written about the importance of good management. In the case of non-profit CCCs, it is even more important that the management team be business oriented as well as mission minded. They should be experienced in retirement home administration and have a successful track record. This is particularly true with a new project. Retirement home administration is a very specialized challenge, and the newer the project, the more it needs an experienced management team.

Some of the problems that inexperienced managers seem to have include tendencies to promise more than they can deliver (to residents, marketing agents, Boards of Directors, etc.), to depend too much on contract services (e.g., farming out food services, housekeeping services, maintenance, etc.), and to be unaware of the many special government regulations that influence such facilities. Church sponsors tend to "save money" by employing nonprofessional management. If a prejudice should exist for church sponsors, they should look for strong "business" leadership in the beginning stages and consider the "charitable" church role after financial stability has been accomplished.

## THE MARKETING PLAN

There are all kinds of marketing experts who are happy to assist a new CCC project. But there are not many who have had experience in the particular challenge that confronts a CCC. Very few projects can be successful without experienced marketing consultation.

In recent years it has become even more important to have a higher requirement of premarketing activity. A larger number of dropouts or a slow fill-up after construction is completed can spell disaster. Preselling of at least 70 percent is a reasonable requirement.

The marketing plan is directly related to the original planning expertise. The demand must be in the near vicinity of the project. The correct (marketable) image must be created from the very beginning. The sponsors cannot invest millions on a gut feeling that the CCC will sell quickly. A CCC that is well-designed and has all other requirements met can still fail miserably if vacancies linger. Premarketing and continued successful marketing cannot be overemphasized.

## CHURCH SPONSORSHIP

The church-sponsored CCC is the ideal kind of sponsorship if the success formula is followed. Even though proprietary ownership is now strongly entering the "industry," the ultimate success of our ministry will depend on our religious-based commitment to service for service's sake.

Because of the unique nature of the CCC facility, the Church may need to depend more and more on existing organizations to lead in future growth efforts. A new, freestanding facility organized by a newly created organization may be taxed beyond its limits, whereas an existing organization can better use its resources of talent and money to meet the unexpected problems. The future will undoubtedly see more merging of our efforts and more "shared management" associations within our Church structure. The key theme of the future will be responsible flexibility and cooperation.

By its very nature, the Church-sponsored CCC is committed to community services (a growing need), has the potential of an army of volunteer services, can develop a charitable image deserving gifts and ongoing support, and can create an endowment base. With these advantages and with the expertise that is available from within our Church, we should be able to look forward to more "booms" and no "busts."

# The Growth of the Multi-Programmed Church Sponsored Long-Term Care Facility

Ronald B. Stuckey

**ABSTRACT.** It is the purpose of this paper to show how long term care facilities can develop into multi-programmed settings. This study examines the structure for developing additional programs and controlling them, while at the same time protecting the assets and viability of each program setting. In addition, it is shown how a single voluntary corporation has been able to sponsor additional community based programs with minimal investment of dollars and personnel.

The matter of providing long term care for the aging has become an area of increasing social concern in recent years, but one complicated by the impacting of several oppositely working factors.

As the nation's population composite grows older, numbers alone sharpen this focus of attention. Fortunately, this development is accompanied by very beneficial advances in medical and social sciences, as related to geriatrics. The picture is badly blurred, however, by the limited number of suitable accommodations and programs available to meet the growing need, and by additional constraints placed upon the existing facilities by social, economic and political forces.

Fewer families care for their elderly at home now than customarily was the case in the past. This trend is toward relying on institutions to provide this care. These establishments are divided between proprietary (for profit) and voluntary (not-for-profit). They include skilled nursing facilities, health related, or intermediate care facilities, adult residences, outpatient programs, day care programs, day

---

Ronald B. Stuckey is Executive Director, Wartburg Lutheran Home for the Aging, Wartburg Nursing Home, Inc., Lutheran Center for the Aging, North Brooklyn Mobile Meals and Lutheran Housing Development Fund Corp. of Long Island, New York.

hospitals, home health services, respite programs, meals on wheels and senior centers. Increasing concern is being focused on programs that will provide alternatives to institutional care.

The purpose of this study is to show how a long term care facility can develop into a multi-program and multi-institutional setting. The paper will provide the history and framework of a particular organization's growth. Future plans will be discussed, and control mechanisms will be examined; problem areas will be identified and issues addressed.

In late 1974, the so-called "nursing home scandals" erupted in the newspapers in New York State. Investigators found numerous instances of poor patient care and financial abuses of the system, which by this time, were funded primarily by Medicaid. It soon became politically popular to characterize nursing homes as warehouses for the elderly, with the sole motivation of operators that of keeping as many elderly persons as possible in institutional settings, in order to maximize profits. At that time, little recognition was given to many voluntary homes that served the elderly for decades prior to the implementation of Medicare and Medicaid. With these new financing mechanisms in place, massive amounts of government funds were made available for caring for the elderly in institutional settings.

The policies of the Wartburg Lutheran Home for the Aging located in Brooklyn, New York, were reviewed in 1975, and the Governing Board determined to extend a commitment to the constituent community to develop and support programs which provided alternatives to institutional care. Programs would be developed within the Home's means to keep elderly clients independent and in the community for as long as possible.

It was determined early in the planning process that as new projects were developed, the financial integrity and viability of existing programs would be protected through the reestablishment of independent not-for-profit corporations under New York State law, and that these corporations, once developed, would exist on the resources and income generated from that program. Separate Governing Boards were established by the membership of the parent corporation.

This led to the development of a strategy which would involve the Wartburg Lutheran Home for the Aging in the development of a number of new corporations for the purpose of providing a variety of service modalities to the aged population of the Greater New York area. The stage was set for the development of a major multi-institutional/multi-programmatic geriatric service complex.

The Wartburg Lutheran Home's history of public services dates back more than a century—to 1875. In that year, a group of eighty-two Lutheran Church members formed a society which would establish a home for elderly persons, known as "The Wartburg Home for the Aged and Infirm." They drafted a Constitution, which, as approved, provided for a twenty-four-member Board of Managers, charged with raising funds with which to purchase property suitable for the purpose.

The following year, a two-story frame house, and an adjoining three story brick building were opened, with twenty-four residents in what was then a rural area of Brooklyn, but, long since built-up, the neighborhood has become known as the East New York Section. Over the years, the Wartburg Lutheran Home for the Aging grew to serve one hundred twenty-three intermediate level, or health related residents. In 1984, ground was broken for a new health related facility to replace some of the original buildings the founders of Wartburg established when they first opened the doors over a hundred years ago. This corporation has evolved as the parent of the other corporations, which have come to be operated under the auspices of the Wartburg Lutheran Home for the Aging.

In 1973, the parent corporation sponsored the Wartburg Nursing Home, a one hundred two bed skilled nursing facility, erected adjacent to the Wartburg Lutheran Home for the Aging. This facility opened in 1973 with funding from the New York State Housing Finance Agency (a "28A Program"). At that time, the two Homes were not fully occupied, serving only one hundred sixty of a potential two hundred twenty-five patients and residents. Also, the Home was suffering under financial burdens imposed by the State's inability to react quickly to the Homes' rate appeals.

In 1974, the Wartburg Lutheran Home for the Aging and Wartburg Nursing Home, Inc. were small facilities in the East New York area without a major financial reserve, facing serious financial difficulties because of problems in reimbursement with the Medicare and Medicaid program. The first job the administrative staff faced was that of reviewing the financial condition of the institution and undertaking steps to strengthen the income and reimbursement from available government and nongovernmental resources. Successful appeals were initiated between 1974 and 1977, strengthening the financial base of the parent institution, enabling it to look ahead to the development of additional programs.

In May of 1977, the Wartburg Lutheran Home for the Aging successfully competed with several other agencies to become the first long term care facility in the New York City area to sponsor a home delivered meals on wheels program. The parent corporation established a new corporation known as North Brooklyn Mobile Meals and received a grant from the New York City Department for the Aging for $216,000 to deliver one hundred fifty homebound meals, five days a week, and to provide social support and recreational opportunities to its clients. This program proved so successful that, currently, two hundred five meals are delivered per day to homes. The facility provides space for the program and administrative backup and accounting support to oversee the operation of this program. The hot meals are prepared and packaged in Wartburg's kitchen prior to shipment to the clients. The facility cooperated with many local community agencies to recruit a Director and to involve members of the local community in the operation of the program. Many persons have been hired from the community to assist in the delivery of the meals. Social support contacts are provided for clients of the program through the use of Senior Aides.

The program spends $375,000 annually to service two hundred five clients plus congregate meals. The cost-effectiveness of the expenditure can best be measured against the cost of institutionalizing those frail, homebound elderly, the only alternative that would be available if no comparable program existed. Using a moderate estimate of $68 per day for health related facility care, the annual cost of institutionalization would be $24,820 per patient, or $5,088,100 to provide custodial care to all recipients. The break even point of the program is fifteen patients, i.e., if only fifteen recipients are prevented from being institutionalized through participation in the program, then the program has paid for itself in terms of taxpayer dollars.

The Smithtown Nursing Home (located in Suffolk County on Long Island), a long term care facility containing two hundred six nursing and one hundred thirty-five health related beds on a twenty-one acre campus, had been operated for approximately seventeen months by the New York State Health Department as a court appointed Receiver, after the former owner was indicted and pleaded guilty to Medicaid fraud. In 1976, the State contacted the Wartburg

Lutheran Home for the Aging to determine whether it would be available to take over the State's court appointed operation as a voluntary receiver.

The Wartburg Board expressed an interest in operating this facility and determined to establish a separate corporation which would then file for a Certificate of Need, as required under the New York State Health Code. The Board determined that the risk of operating this facility, with a seven million dollar budget, was one that had to be accomplished through an independent corporate structure. The Wartburg parent corporation would not be able to guarantee large losses which might be incurred by this corporation in the event of a crisis with Medicaid and Medicare mechanisms.

The Board also recognized that some capital funds would need to be raised to provide capital for the operation of a new facility. After several months of addressing various Church bodies, foundations and individuals, the parent corporation was able to identify a donor, who provided the Wartburg Lutheran Home for the Aging with a gift of $250,000, which was to be controlled by the parent corporation and used to guarantee a line of credit to serve the new corporation.

The New York State Health Department investigated the character and competence of the Board of the new corporation, and determined that this new corporation was capable of operating the Smithtown Nursing Home as a receivership corporation.

This Board then entered into negotiations with the bank holding company which held a defaulted mortgage in excess of six million dollars on the long term care facility. It was agreed that the Board would enter into a fifteen-year lease which would enable the banks to recover their initial mortgage loan during the time of lease operation. In addition, the banking group agreed to advance $1,100,000 so the new operators might correct a variety of previously identified physical plant and life safety deficiencies. It was also agreed that at the end of the fifteen years, the New York State Health Department would establish a purchase price, which the banking group would honor, based upon the reimbursement principles at that time. The banking group would provide the operator with a 100% mortgage in order that the loan might be paid off in a manner consistent with reimbursement principles. In summary, the new corporation, after fifteen years of leasing the facility and operating it as the Lutheran Center for the Aging, would then take title to the property and own the physical plant.

The Lutheran Center for the Aging operated the first sixteen months as a voluntary receiver. During this time, the Certificate of Need application was approved and the receivership was terminated. The Lutheran Center became a formally established long term care facility operating as a distinct not-for-profit corporation under New York State laws.

In summary, the Lutheran Center for the Aging was assured that after investing a number of years of work and considerable dollars in this new facility, it would have the opportunity to ultimately control the property through ownership in a manner that might not otherwise be available. It also resulted in a policy of providing a mechanism for shifting long term care beds from proprietary to not-for-profit sponsorship.

It was also recognized that construction of a new three hundred forty-one bed facility in today's dollars would require an investment of approximately fifteen to eighteen million dollars. In addition, it would have been almost impossible to get a Certificate of Need approved for three hundred forty-one new long term care beds under the existing State policies.

The State also agreed to allow the new corporation to use receivables accrued under its court appointed operation to assist in initial cash flow problems. Within the first week of operation, payroll expenses exceeded $80,000 for more than three hundred employees. The Department of Social Services agreed to an accelerated payment schedule for several months until the operation was functioning under its own momentum.

To date the corporation has been able to turn the facility's very negative public image around to the point where the community is very actively involved. The facility staff have received numerous awards, including a recent prestigious National Award for its Therapeutic Drama Programs, involving residents of the facility and their performances for the community. The Volunteer Department is very active, utilizing the services of adult as well as teenage volunteers in a year-round program to enhance the quality of life for residents.

In 1983 at Lutheran Center we were successful in implementing a bed conversion. We now have eighty health related beds and two hundred sixty-one much needed skilled nursing beds. Also, in 1983 our Long Term Home Health Care Program was opened to serve the elderly of the community, enabling them to be serviced at home instead of being institutionalized. We expect to open a Day Care

Program the latter part of this year. We also sponsor Life-Line. Adapters are installed on the telephones of our Long Term Home Health Care patients, and, should an emergency arise, the person need only to press a buzzer to be connected with our switchboard from where immediate assistance will be sent.

At the time negotiations were taking place to develop the Lutheran Center for the Aging in Smithtown, it was recognized that housing for the elderly was becoming an urgent need in this Long Island community. A recent not-for-profit housing program for senior citizens, involving approximately three hundred apartments, had resulted in more than two thousand applications for the existing units. It was initially determined that the vacant land on the site of Lutheran Center for the aging might be a good site to provide housing under HUD's #202 Program. This program provides a construction grant of 100% to build apartments, with a mortgage to be repaid over forty years.

The sponsoring corporation of Wartburg Lutheran Home for the Aging formed a new corporation, known at the Lutheran Housing Development Fund of Long Island under the New York State housing laws as a not-for-profit corporation.

The Board of the Lutheran Housing Development Fund soon determined that the Town regulations would not permit construction of a large number of apartments on the land available at the site of the Lutheran Center to make the project feasible. Application was made to HUD under the #202 program to build one hundred-thirteen apartments for seniors, with Section 8 subsidy funds available. The parent corporation committed the initial $10,000 required for the project to the new corporation. Approximately six months after the application was submitted, HUD notified Lutheran Housing Development Fund, and its sponsor, that they were the recipients of $3,500,000 for the construction of senior housing. Ultimately $5,672,000 was made available for apartments of 640 square feet per unit.

During this time, the Board had been searching for an adequate alternative site for the project. Following the receipt of the funds, the Board approached HUD to determine if a change in site could be made. The Board was able to locate a thirty-nine acre tract of land in the adjacent community of Kings Park for construction of the housing units. An agreement was entered into with the owner of the land on a contingency basis, and an architect and attorney were employed, also on a contingency basis, to develop the required agreements and plans in order to receive a Conditional Commitment from HUD.

Extensive negotiations were entered into with the Town in order to resolve the many complex issues raised by the Planning Department and the Town Board. These problems were resolved almost a year later. In February, 1983, the groundbreaking ceremony took place, and in May, 1984, we dedicated our housing complex, which we named the Martin Luther Terrace Apartments. Our housing units are fully occupied, with over one thousand on the waiting list.

At the present time, Wartburg Lutheran Home for the Aging, through its parent corporation and its subsidiary corporations, has provided a means to serve more than one thousand elderly persons within the communities identified as our service area. The organization has grown since 1974 from two small institutions serving approximately one hundred sixty persons to a multi-institutional/multi-programmatic conglomerate under independent corporate structures operating combined budgets in excess of twenty million dollars, and employing more than seven hundred people to care for the clients entrusted to them.

Other plans include exploring relationships with Stony Brook University so that we might ultimately provide a setting to implement Dr. Robert Butler's concept of "The Teaching Nursing Home." We already provide internships for students in Physical Therapy, Social Services, Activities and Administration, to be placed in our facilities in order to be trained in a geriatric setting. Our present multi-institutional system of care provides a number of benefits for both the patient, in terms of providing a higher level of care, the community, in terms of providing less expensive alternatives to the more expensive institutional care, and to the organizations which might not otherwise be available to a single smaller unit. Our multi-institutional arrangement has already provided numerous opportunities for managerial and support personnel to assist in times of emergencies involving labor stoppages, disasters, such as floods and snowstorms, and for special programs, such as the Golden Olympics.

The multi-institutional/multi-programmatic organization has a number of opportunities for providing controls within and between organizations through a central administrative structure. As noted earlier, separate corporations were established by the parent in order to protect the financial integrity of each program. The membership of the parent corporation elects the Governing Boards of each subsidiary corporation. A single Executive Director is employed by the organization to act as Chief Executive Officer, responsible to the Board and responsible for operational aspects of the corporations. The Boards set policy for the programs and monitor the financial operations of each program. They carry fiduciary responsibility for the assets of the corporation. They do not become involved in the internal operation of the individual program.

The Executive Director is responsible for interpreting the policies of the Board, hiring administrative and financial staff to operate each of the programs, overseeing the financial operations of the corporations, and providing leadership in the areas of planning and development.

The administrator of each of the programs is responsible to the Executive Director. The Fiscal Director reports directly to the Executive Director. The parent corporation also employs a Development Officer who reports to the Executive Director.

The financial operations of the various corporations are centralized at the Long Island facility. Plans are under way to complete computerization of all the accounting functions of the corporations. A centralized office staff maintains responsibility for the day to day accounting and bookkeeping operations.

The growth of our multi-institutional program has enabled us to serve a much larger client population with rather limited resources and assets. Inherent in this concept is the need for not-for-profit institutions to imaginatively develop new programs using existing resources without allowing these resources and assets to disappear. This means new programs must be able to generate support income.

Some of the benefits the organization derives through its multi-institutional approach are:

1. Stronger and larger organizations are better able to respond to pressures from regulatory and reimbursement agencies than smaller, independent ones. In some cases, size plays a very positive role in an organization's ability to attract the attention of a regulatory or reimbursement agency. Failure of the agency to respond to an organization's problem might result in a program failure which could not be tolerated in the community.
2. Future managerial staff can be developed. As an organization grows, career ladder opportunities develop for promotion from within.

3. The independence of each of the programs strengthens the others because the failure of one program will not destroy the others.
4. A certain amount of healthy competition exists between the organizations. A different organization can cope with labor emergencies in times of crisis by drawing on resources from other related organizations. The abilities to draw on additional managerial staff in times of crisis has strengthened this organization on several occasions.
5. Certain functions, such as finances, purchasing, pharmacy and others can be done at a central location without duplicating staff. This has resulted in financial savings for the institution.

A number of programs face cutbacks in the next several years because of budget tightening and cost containment from federal and state agencies. Centralized planning has taken place at the management level so that the organization is prepared for cutbacks. A program of cost containment has been implemented. The growth of programs, with very limited start-up resources, has always required prudent managers. A number of concepts and assumptions will be severely tested in the next five years as we continue to strengthen existing programs, replace physical plant and review future growth.

# Modernizing Organizational Structures for Agencies and Institutions to Meet New Governmental and Economic Challenges

Dar W. Vriesman

**ABSTRACT.** The Church's agencies and institutions must respond to the challenge of serving an increasing number of elderly people. Lower levels of government assistance, competition for available funds by proprietary organizations, and a burgeoning aged population are present societal conditions calling for board and management staff action. Strategic planning, political activity, and possibly corporate restructuring are alternatives to be considered. The benefits gained by such organizational moves come in the form of operational strengths, flexibility in the market, and efficiency in and acceptance of programs. In turn, agencies and institutions help assure their social ministry role in future years.

Based on Christ's commission to care for people in need, the Lutheran Church is presently much involved in both formal and informal networks to meet the challenge of one particular needy persons classification—the elderly. While not all older people fit into a formal network dedicated to caring for them, there are many who do. Thus, the Church has created social ministry agencies and institutions having definite, formal, and well-planned services for the aged who are unable in many ways to care for themselves.

Church-related social ministry organizations, however, have the obligation to look beyond their present day-to-day functions. They need to adopt modern management policies and procedures in order to assure their future operation in the field for which they are commissioned. Thus, as agencies and institutions develop new structures and programs, they will be better able to respond to existing and future needs in the elderly market.

---

Dar W. Vriesman is with St. John's Lutheran Home, Mars, Pennsylvania.

One approach to fulfilling this obligation is the concern of this paper. The great commission of compassion remains the same—the milieu is what has changed—and that change calls for new flexibility and adaptability in social ministry organizations.

## SOME CAUSES

Setting aside ever-present but often politically motivated blame-assigning statements on the subject, objective social studies have indicated that government programs for the elderly could not continue in the manner in which they were financed in the late 1970s. While appropriate levels of federal and state funding for social welfare efforts will always be a matter of personal philosophy, government balance sheets began to indicate the insolvency of such efforts was a real possibility during the 1980 decade.

Kerschner (1984, p. 20) indicated to the 26th Annual Meeting and Conference of American Association Homes for the Aging,

> . . . for the increasing numbers of elderly people in our land, when it comes to health care, Americans believe that price is no object. In short, we treat health care as if it were free. Thus, Medicare costs are going up. By the end of this decade the program will be in the red and by 1995 it will have a deficit exceeding $300 billion. At the present rate, the program's costs will double every five years. That presents the government with some stark choices. It can either double the health insurance fund tax rate every five years, slash Medicare benefits, or try to control the rate of increase in all healthcare related programs. Higher deductibles, higher premiums and high new copayments are the kinds of proposals that have been made in Washington to reduce the cost of Medicare and to some extent Medicaid.

Thus, the first observation is that while there are more elderly American people who are potentially in need of additional services and care, there are fewer dollars per capita available from government sources. Social ministry organizations need to face those facts.

A second reason for church-related organizations to be concerned about their current status and the continuation of their ability to provide care for the elderly is the competition provided by proprietary organizations. Because of rapidly changing numbers, it is impossible to provide complete and accurate statistics on the percentage of hospital beds, nursing home facilities, and other human services controlled by the for-profit sector of the economy.

A short scenario is sufficient to describe the situation. Because of the essential nature of health and human services in a free economy, it is understandable that besides physicians, other providers may work to produce income by answering these needs. Motivated by making profit from such work, proprietary companies control an increasing major-percentage of the industry. Certainly, many of these organizations offer high-quality programs. Yet, based on the reasons for their existence, these companies care primarily for those who are able to provide sufficient revenue for services rendered to them. Also, market dominance is often important in order that there can be both control and economies of scale. Add to these facts about proprietaries, a dynamic flexibility made possible from capital provided by investors and both the negative and positive impact of competitive fee-for-service organizations can be appreciated.

A third reason for church-related social ministry agencies and institutions to rethink their structure and operations is almost paradoxical. It is the rapid expansion of the elderly market and the needs identified therein which may be so numerous they are possibly beyond the capabilities of the church-related organizations created to serve such people. In everyday terms—business may be too good!

Louden (1984, p. 15) has observed that "the aging trends in our society portend of greater demands not only for housing but for health care and a full range of other services. Obviously this will attract a lot of competition in that market place." But are church organizations ready for that kind of competition—and are they prepared to minister to a vast number of poor people that such competition may leave without services?

Louden (1984, p. 16) questions the needs of the elderly market. "To what segment of the population are social ministry organizations gearing their efforts? What is the source of income for that segment? What is the poverty rate amongst those to be served? What is the activity limitation? What are the morbidity rates in the population to be served? What are the levels of education to be encountered as services are delivered to the needy people?" The needs will be there—again, the question is whether they may overwhelm those commissioned to help but not adequately prepared to respond?

In summary—an awareness of the aging population by church-related agencies and institutions continues; the elderly will present increasing needs both in type and number; there is competition to meet such needs; but there is a serious drop-off in available financial sources to cover the cost of serving the aged population.

## MEANINGFUL AND EFFECTIVE RESPONSES

Because of the cause and effect relationship—and, hopefully, based also on a desire to use the best of the present state-of-the-management art in their endeavors—it is essential that social ministry organizations consider at least three serious methods to address the continuing fulfillment of their responsibilities, now and in the future.

### Strategic Planning

Ever since the essential components of good management were identified, it has been recognized that planning is the first step toward the desired successful outcome of any project. However, either because boards and staff of church-related organizations and institutions were not aware that good management techniques could be applied to Christian endeavors or because they were convinced that Providential guidance would take care of everything, planning was often an unheard of component in many such operations.

Recently, people-businesses have joined product-producers in recognizing that the continued life of a corporation goes beyond the vision of one or two special leaders. Thus, they have given attention to the practice of ongoing good management techniques including planning. First called long-range planning, over the last few years strategic planning has become the term assigned to this essential ingredient of well-run organizations.

Strategic planning must be based on a number of essential concepts before it can be an integral part and a benefit to the dynamic social ministry organization. Taking seriously the advice to prepare for the future by planning ahead, it must not be understood as crystal-ball gazing. Future developments can be anticipated based upon the gathering and evaluation of historical and current data. Taking positive action in the present has a lot to do with determining the future. In order to deliver services successfully (i.e., meeting identified needs with meaningful and satisfactory services), organizations must plan strategically; they need to anticipate what the market will be like in five, ten, or even twenty years. As church-related agencies and institutions use a definite planning process to determine where they want to be in the forthcoming years, it will also become clear that there will always be a place for the well-managed, strategically-placed, nonprofit organization.

Two important concerns usually emerge from strategic planning in agencies and institutions. They relate directly to the aforementioned reasons for instigating such planning and deserve serious attention.

## Political Involvement

In modern America, most social ministry organizations are dependent upon government sources for some portion of their funding. Because of this, the strategic planning process ought to alert board and staff members to the necessity of becoming active in the political arena.

Hastings, Oldaker, and Kerman (1984, p. 80) indicated

It is naive to imagine that political activity should be avoided because it may be construed as being somehow illegal. And, even though a few 501(c)3 organizations and institutions now do engage in some form of lobbying (either directly or through affiliated organizations) many seem to think that they are certainly prohibited from participating in election-related activities. In fact they are not. Not-for-profit, tax-exempt organizations can affect electoral politics. There can be direct action and activities through PACs.

Some basic steps of becoming involved in the politics of operating a social ministry organization are as follows: (a) the development of a mission statement that includes political awareness and action; (b) addressing political issues directly in the strategic planning process; (c) budgeting sufficient funds for activity in this area; (d) creating a board level political relations/action committee; (e) keeping employees and clients and responsible parties informed on government matters; (f) inviting legislative persons to events and meetings; (g) contacting political decision makers at all levels by phone, telegrams, and letters.

## Corporate Reorganization

Strategic planning must bring to question to those who control organizations serving the aged, the effectiveness of its present corporate structure. Concern about the changes in the human services/healthcare environment and the challenges and opportunities for the future they bring ought to cause organization leaders to recognize three key points (McCormick and Frado, 1983, p. 21): (a) they probably cannot rely solely on existing services as their primary sustenance source, (b) freely given or less-than-cost charges for services rendered is a policy that will have a difficult time surviving in today's and tomorrow's highly regulated world, (c) those organizations adaptable to change have a greater likelihood of survival.

Based on these considerations, alert boards and administration staffs will respond by developing strategic objectives that result in diversified human service roles. Then their organizations (particularly present single-purpose institutions) will reexamine the requirements of the corporate structure to achieve these objectives. Thus, the possibility of corporate reorganization originates with strategic planning, and it may become the means to a desired end—that of better achieving the organization's strategic objectives.

Gerber (1981) points out that consideration of restructuring should rest on certain basic principles. They include the following:

1. Reorganization is not an evasion of the law. It is, if properly planned and implemented, an avoidance of the law. There is nothing wrong with avoidance. Americans are not required to plan activities to bring them within the scope of every conceivable law which may be applicable to them.
2. Restructuring is not a sham because such a goal must have substance and all those associated with the organization must accept the realities of that substance and conform to it.
3. Board members of not-for-profit corporations are fiduciaries. As such, they have a duty to protect the assets of their organization. Consideration of restructuring and implementation *when appropriate* is consistent with, and is in furtherance of this duty.
4. Restructuring is not right for everyone.

Gerber also suggests the following goals that may be used to test the feasibility of the corporate restructuring endeavor: (a) sheltering assets from governmental intervention, (b) improving outside re-imbursement, (c) improving tax consequences, (d) improving cer-tificate of need status, (e) increasing efficiency of organizational operations, (f) increasing operating flexibility, (g) protecting assets from malpractice claims, (h) increasing church and community in-volvement, (i) facilitating generation of additional revenues, (j) sur-viving in a competitive market place.

Where does a social ministry organization plan to go in the future? Certainly it is necessary for it to consider new activities in order to better meet the emerging needs of its constituents; that goal is made possible by remaining flexible enough to assure its con-tinued existence.

## BENEFICIAL EFFECTS

The concept of the Church fulfilling the command of the Lord to care for the elderly through its social ministry organizations is basic. Now the contemporary society needs contemporary agencies and in-stitutions utilizing modern management structures and procedures in order to accomplish their goals. And it is very important—that when organizations are operated in this manner, its target population is better served.

When utilizing the strategic planning process, board members, employed staff, volunteers, supporting congregations and the com-munity know more about an organization's programs and its needs. This is so because integral to a properly-done planning program are two ingredients: (a) a broad base of knowledgeable help to make the resulting plan reliable and representative, and (b) the concern for an organization's future by a group of individuals does much to assure its continued existence.

From the political activity generated by the planning process, there comes mutual appreciation from an agency or institution and government representatives. That is, both legislators and officials come to know the organization as a valuable service provider. Assuming a positive and supportive attitude, politicians may use social ministry people in a consulting role early in the legislation or rule-making processes.

The demographics of society indicate that the needs of the elder-ly will continue to call from the market place to the Church for assistance during many years to come. Being positioned, structured, and operated in a way to answer that call is the obligation of every church-related agency and institution that is concerned about Christ's commission to serve his elderly people.

## REFERENCES

Gerber, L. Adapting to regulations and the marketplace. *Hospital Financial Management,* August 1981, 12-15.

Hastings, D. A., Oldaker, W. C., and Kerman, L. J. Tax exempt hospitals and electoral politics. *Hospitals,* August 1, 1984, 80-82.

Kerschner, P. Medicare and medicaid at the crossroads. *Communities that Care,* 1984, 19-23.

Louden, T. The aging of America: Implications for corporate strategy. *Communities that Care,* 1984, 15-18.

McCormick, T. and Frado, R. Corporate reorganization: a cast study. *Hospital Health Services Administration,* 1983, 28, 21-29.